LIVING THROUGH

WORLD WAR I

Nicola Barber

www.raintreepublishers.co.uk
Visit our website to find out more information about Raintree books.

To order:
☎ Phone 0845 6044371
🖨 Fax +44 (0) 1865 312263
📠 Email myorders@raintreepublishers.co.uk

Customers from outside the UK please telephone +44 1865 312262

Raintree is an imprint of Capstone Global Library Limited, a company incorporated in England and Wales having its registered office at 7 Pilgrim Street, London, EC4V 6LB – Registered company number: 6695582

Edited by Andrew Farrow, Laura Knowles, and Megan Cotugno
Designed by Steve Mead
Original illustrations © Capstone Global Library Ltd
Picture research by Ruth Blair
Production by Eirian Griffiths
Originated by Capstone Global Library Ltd
Printed and bound in China by Leo Paper Group Ltd

ISBN 978 1 406 23490 9 (hardback)
15 14 13 12 11
10 9 8 7 6 5 4 3 2 1

ISBN 978 1 406 23498 5 (paperback)
16 15 14 13 12
10 9 8 7 6 5 4 3 2 1

British Library Cataloguing in Publication Data
Barber, Nicola.
Living through World War I.
940.3-dc22
A full catalogue record for this book is available from the British Library.

Acknowledgements
We would like to thank the following for permission to reproduce photographs: akg-images pp. 5, 43 (ullstein bild), 56; © Corbis p. 32; Corbis pp. 10 (© Bettmann), 15 (© Hulton-Deutsch Collection), 26 (© Bettmann), 28 (© Bettmann), 35 (© Hulton-Deutsch Collection), 49 (© Hulton-Deutsch Collection), 51 (© Bettmann), 53 (© Bettmann), 54 (© K.J. Historical), 59 (© Bettmann); Getty images pp. 17 (Hulton Archive), 25 (Hulton Archive), 30 (Buyenlarge), 41 (George C. Beresford/Stringer), 45 (Time Life Pictures/Mansell); Mary Evans pp. 9, 37, 46; National Library of Australia p. 21; Photo library pp. 61 (The Print Collector), 62 (The Print Collector).

Cover photograph of a British solider eating his dinner in the trenches during World War I reproduced with the permission of Corbis/ © Underwood & Underwood.

We would like to thank A P Watt Ltd for their permission on behalf of The Literary Executors of the Estate of H G Wells to reproduce an extract from H G Wells, *The War That Will End War* (Frank & Cecil Palmer, 1914) on p. 17.

We would like to thank John Allen Williams for his invaluable help in the preparation of this book.

Every effort has been made to contact copyright holders of any material reproduced in this book. Any omissions will be rectified in subsequent printings if notice is given to the publisher.

Disclaimer
All the Internet addresses (URLs) given in this book were valid at the time of going to press. However, due to the dynamic nature of the Internet, some addresses may have changed, or sites may have changed or ceased to exist since publication. While the author and publisher regret any inconvenience this may cause readers, no responsibility for any such changes can be accepted by either the author or the publisher.

CONTENTS

THE WAR'S ORIGINS 4

1914 10

THE DARDANELLES AND GALLIPOLI 18

THE EASTERN FRONT 22

THE WAR AT SEA 28

THE WESTERN FRONT 34

THE CHANGING NATURE OF WARFARE 42

THE USA ENTERS THE WAR 48

THE HOME FRONT 54

THE END OF THE WAR 60

WHAT HAVE WE LEARNED? 66

TIMELINE 68

GLOSSARY 70

NOTES ON SOURCES 73

BIBLIOGRAPHY 76

FIND OUT MORE 77

INDEX 79

Words printed in **bold** are explained in the glossary.

THE WAR'S ORIGINS

In 1871, Otto von Bismarck, then prime minister of Prussia, achieved his life-long ambition. The Franco-Prussian War was the last in a series of wars and campaigns that resulted in Bismarck's dream of creating a unified Germany. Under the **treaty** that ended the war, France lost the territories of Alsace and Lorraine to Germany, and this caused deep and continuing resentment amongst the French.[1] The German Empire was established with Bismarck as its chancellor and Wilhelm I of Prussia as its Kaiser (emperor). The rise of a united Germany sparked new rivalries that laid the seeds for World War I – a war whose outcome still influences world events today.

ALLIANCES AND TREATIES

The other European powers at the time – Austria-Hungary, Britain, France, and Russia – regarded this new empire with some unease. Bismarck, meanwhile, embarked on a new policy to protect Germany and to maintain peace in Europe. One of his concerns was the **Balkans**. Not only was the rule of the **Ottoman Empire** being challenged by **nationalist** movements, but both Austria-Hungary and Russia were trying to gain power in the region. Another worry was France – Bismarck knew that one day the French would seek revenge for their humiliating defeat in 1871.

Bismarck's solution was to make **alliances** to try to isolate France. He signed agreements with Austria-Hungary in 1879, and with both Austria-Hungary and Italy in 1882 (the Triple Alliance). Bismarck knew that any alliance between France and Russia would be particularly dangerous for Germany. If there was a war, Germany would be forced to fight on two fronts at once. Therefore, in 1887, he negotiated a secret treaty with Russia (the Reinsurance Treaty).[2]

WILHELM'S *WELTPOLITIK*

In 1888, Wilhelm II succeeded his grandfather as Kaiser of the German Empire. Wilhelm II had little time for Bismarck's cautious strategy of diplomacy and secrecy, and he forced the chancellor to resign in 1890. Wilhelm had already decided not to renew the

Reinsurance Treaty with Russia. This opened the way for Russia to form a new alliance with France, which it promptly did in 1894. Wilhelm's vision was for Germany to become a major global power through a policy known as *Weltpolitik* (world policy). In pursuit of this policy Wilhelm wanted to acquire territories overseas as German **colonies**. He also decided to build a German navy that would rival that of Britain in size and strength (see pages 8–9). In these aims, Kaiser Wilhelm was backed up by his new chancellor, Bernhard von Bülow, and his naval adviser, Alfred von Tirpitz.

BIOGRAPHY

Otto von Bismarck

1815–1898

BORN: Prussia

ROLE: Prime minister of Prussia, and imperial chancellor (1871–1890). He was responsible for uniting most German-speaking kingdoms and states in Europe into one empire. As imperial chancellor, his aim was to maintain peace in Europe to allow the new German Empire to flourish.

DID YOU KNOW?

Bismarck introduced the first social security scheme in Europe, including insurance for workers against accidents, sickness, and old age. He had a political motive, though. His motive was fear of the rise of **socialism** in Germany. These schemes were designed to stop people from joining the increasingly popular socialist parties.

IMPERIALISM

The end of the 19th and beginning of the 20th centuries saw an upsurge in **imperialism**, as European powers scrambled to gain control of overseas colonies, mainly in Africa and Asia. Imperialism is the dominance of a powerful state over another, usually weaker, state, often by use of military force. Some countries were already established imperial powers. By the 19th century, Britain, for example, had an empire that included colonies in Australia, India, and North America. Its empire gave Britain a huge commercial advantage. Not only were its colonies sources of cheap raw materials, they also provided ready markets for goods manufactured in Britain. To maintain this commercial advantage, Britain had a powerful navy to patrol the world's seas and oceans. Throughout the 19th century, Britain remained in "splendid isolation", unwilling to become involved in alliances with other European powers.

The turn of the 19th century saw Britain's supremacy and isolation being challenged. Other countries wanted overseas colonies. Germany, Italy, Belgium, the United States, and Japan all joined in the rush to lay claim to parts of Africa and Asia.[3] Germany was not alone in building a naval fleet to rival that of Britain. France, Japan, and the United States built up large navies of their own. In 1902, Britain signed its first international alliance with Japan, followed in 1904 by a treaty with France (the *"Entente Cordiale"*) and, in 1907, one with Russia.[4]

SUSPICION AND CRISES

Britain's international alliances were made primarily to safeguard its colonies. Amongst other issues, the Anglo-Japanese treaty addressed British fears about its commercial interests in the Far East. The *Entente Cordiale* cleared up disputes over territories in Africa – Britain kept its claim over Egypt, while France kept its control over Morocco. But in Germany, Kaiser Wilhelm viewed these new alliances with great suspicion. The Anglo-Russian agreement of 1907, which aimed to settle disputes over territorial claims in Persia (Iran), Tibet, and Afghanistan, only made Germany feel more encircled. Two rival **power blocs** were emerging in Europe, the Triple Entente (Britain, France, and Russia) and the Triple Alliance (Germany, Austria-Hungary, and Italy).

In 1908, trouble erupted in the Balkans when Austria-Hungary took control of the provinces of Bosnia and Herzegovina. This act was greeted with outrage both in the neighbouring country of Serbia, and in Russia, which backed Serbia. In 1911, a crisis in Morocco further highlighted the tensions between the European powers. Germany sent a gunboat into the port of Agadir in Morocco to challenge French supremacy in the region. The confrontation was eventually resolved diplomatically.

European attention moved quickly back to the Balkans. War broke out in 1912, when an alliance made up of Bulgaria, Serbia, Greece, and Montenegro (the Balkan League) finally brought about the end of Ottoman (Turk) rule in Europe. However, the treaty that ended the war pleased none of the members of the Balkan League. War broke out again in 1913 when Bulgaria attacked Serbia. This ended with Serbia making considerable territorial gains.

△ The Balkan Wars resulted in the Ottoman Empire losing most of its European territories.

THE NAVAL ARMS RACE

Kaiser Wilhelm II desired the prestige and commercial advantages of an overseas empire. In order to acquire and maintain far-flung colonies he needed a powerful navy. But both Wilhelm and his naval adviser, Alfred von Tirpitz, knew that Germany could not build a navy to equal the power and size of the British fleet. Instead, Tirpitz proposed the "risk theory". In this, Germany would build a navy large enough to pose a risk to the British in battle, and therefore to deter Britain from going to war with Germany.[5] Tirpitz thought that the presence of a large German fleet would be enough to increase Germany's maritime influence and allow the Kaiser to "conduct a great overseas policy".[6]

GERMAN CONSTRUCTION

The First German Naval Bill was passed in 1897. It provided for the construction of 19 battleships, 12 large cruisers, 30 small cruisers, and assorted smaller ships. A second bill passed in 1900 doubled the number of battleships to be built.[7] Another development was the construction of the Kiel Canal, a waterway to link the Baltic Sea and the North Sea. It was officially opened in 1895 by Wilhelm II. Between 1907 and 1914, the canal was widened to allow the biggest of the new German battleships to pass along it.[8] The canal proved a vital link for the German Baltic and North Sea fleets.

BRITAIN'S RESPONSE

Britain's response to all of this German activity was to reinforce and reorganize its own navy. It was now safe to return several ships from the Pacific to boost naval defences in waters nearer home, thanks to the Anglo-Japanese treaty of 1902. These reforms were carried out under the leadership of Admiral Sir John Fisher, who became First Sea Lord in 1904.[9] Fisher was also responsible for the construction of the world's first "all-big-gun" battleship, HMS *Dreadnought*.

The construction of the *Dreadnought* was completed in December 1906. This battleship was faster and armed with bigger guns than any previous battleships. It immediately made all the existing ships in the British and German navies out-of-date and obsolete. Kaiser Wilhelm recognized that HMS *Dreadnought* was the "armament of the future".[10] The race was now on to produce more of this powerful new type of ship. HMS *Dreadnought* gave its name to this new class of battleship.

Germany secretly launched its own **dreadnought** programme in June 1906.[11] In 1908, Britain discovered that Germany was in the process of building four dreadnoughts, while only two were under construction for the British navy. The British government and navy chiefs disagreed about committing large amounts of money to dreadnought construction. The navy wanted to build six dreadnoughts, while the government wanted only four, with four more later, if needed. The British press stirred up patriotic fervour with slogans, such as "We want eight and we won't wait".[12] All eight dreadnoughts were eventually built.

HMS *Dreadnought*

In service: 1906–1918   *Length:* 160.6m (527ft)

Beam (width): 25m (82ft)   *Crew:* 773

Speed: 21 knots   *Armament:* 305mm (10 x 12in.) guns

Active service: On 29 March 1915 HMS *Dreadnought* rammed and sank the German submarine U-29.

You can find out more about this ship by visiting www.royal-navy.mod.uk/history/ships and clicking on "HMS *Dreadnought* 1906".

▷ HMS *Dreadnought* was built in Portsmouth dock in just over a year, 1905–1906.

1914

In the summer of 1914, Archduke Franz Ferdinand, the nephew of the Austrian emperor Franz Josef I, decided to visit the Bosnian capital, Sarajevo. Bosnia had been under Austria-Hungarian rule since 1908 (see page 7). This caused great resentment amongst many Bosnians. The **annexation** of Bosnia had prompted a rapid growth in terrorist groups, particularly amongst Serb nationalists who were dedicated to the overthrow of Austrian rule.[1] For the Serb population in Bosnia, the date of Franz Ferdinand's visit, 28 June, was an unfortunate choice.[2] In the Serbian calendar 28 June is Vidovdan, a national festival that commemorates a famous battle fought between the Serbs and the Turks in the 14th century.[3] Austrian diplomats warned Franz Ferdinand that he would be in grave danger if he visited Sarajevo on such a significant day, but the warnings were ignored.[4]

△ This is Archduke Franz Ferdinand and his wife, Sophie, in Sarajevo on 28 June 1914, pictured about an hour before they were both assassinated.

On the morning of 28 June, Franz Ferdinand and his wife, Sophie, paraded through the streets of Sarajevo in an open-topped car. At one point, the car took a wrong turn and was forced to stop. A young man named Gavrilo Princep saw his chance. Stepping out of the crowd, he shot and killed both the Archduke and his wife. Princep had links with the nationalist movement "Young Bosnia" and with a secret organization based in Serbia, known as the "Black Hand". The death of Franz Ferdinand and his wife caused fury in Austria-Hungary. Although the Serbian government had nothing to do with the plot, the terrorists' involvement with the Black Hand gave Austria-Hungary the excuse it had long been looking for to assert its authority over Serbia.

A CHAIN OF EVENTS

Austria-Hungary consulted with its ally, Germany. Kaiser Wilhelm II promised to "stand behind" Austria-Hungary in its actions against Serbia. Germany expected such a war to be a localized affair, but it was prepared to take the risk of a full-scale European war. On 23 July 1914, Austria-Hungary issued Serbia with an ultimatum. Acting on the belief that Serbia was involved in the Sarajevo plot, the ultimatum made ten demands aimed at ending Serbian terrorist activity. Serbia agreed to nearly all the demands. But Austria-Hungary was adamant that Serbia must accept the whole document. On 28 July 1914, Austria-Hungary declared war on Serbia.[5]

Russia didn't have a treaty with Serbia, but it was bound to its Serbian neighbours by strong religious and historical ties,[6] and was concerned about increased Austro-Hungarian influence in the Balkans. The Russian **tsar** and government knew they could not stand and watch Serbia being bullied by Austria-Hungary. Russia was already prepared for war. When Austro-Hungarian forces began to bombard Serbia's capital, Belgrade, Russia announced the **mobilization** of its army, although it still hoped for a negotiated settlement.

Table of military strength of European states in 1914[7]

Country	Population	Mobilized army
Austria-Hungary	49,800,000	2,000,000
Germany	65,000,000	4,500,000
Russia	167,000,000	4,500,000
France	39,600,000	3,780,000
Britain	46,400,000	713,514

Germany viewed Russian mobilization as an act of aggression, and in any case, was required militarily to mobilize its forces if Russia did. If Germany did not, it would have no time to stop a Russian invasion. Even though Russia still hoped for a peaceful settlement, Germany declared war on Russia on 1 August. At that point, Germany's military plan, the Schlieffen Plan (see panel below), came into operation. Although the perceived threat to Germany was coming from Russia in the east, the first step of this plan was a rapid attack on France, in the west, through Belgium. On 2 August, therefore, Belgium received an ultimatum from Germany demanding that it allow safe passage across its territory for the German army. As a **neutral** country, Belgium refused. On 3 August, Germany declared war on France. That same night, the German army invaded Belgium.

The Schlieffen Plan

Named after the man who developed it, Count Alfred von Schlieffen, this military plan was the German response to the alliance between France and Russia of 1894 (see page 5). Germany feared a war on two fronts, against France in the west and Russia in the east, and this alliance sharpened that fear. Schlieffen knew that in the event of war, the mobilization of the Russian army would take several weeks (see page 22). His plan was to make use of this time to crush the French army, before concentrating forces in the east. Instead of attacking France along the heavily fortified French-German border, Schlieffen planned to send the German army on a rapid march through Belgium, which was a neutral country, and then swing south into France to capture Paris.[8]

The German attack on Belgium forced Britain to commit itself for the first time. Up until that point the British Foreign Secretary, Sir Edward Grey, had been working to end the crisis through mediation and diplomacy. But German violation of Belgium's neutrality changed the situation, because British leaders had long felt they could not permit such a powerful country to control the territory just across the narrow strait from them. Although Britain had no formal agreement with any country to involve it in the war, it did have a treaty (dating back to 1839) which committed Britain to Belgium's defence if that country was invaded. Britain declared war on Germany on 4 August. In a matter of a few weeks, Europe had descended into war. Serbia, the initial cause of the crisis, was almost forgotten.

This map shows the planned movements of the French armies, known as Plan XVII, and of Germany's Schlieffen Plan.

Planned advance by German armies
Planned advance by French armies
Fortified areas

THE BATTLE OF THE FRONTIERS

Speed of attack was central to the Schlieffen Plan. The plan was put into effect not by Schlieffen, who had retired in 1906, but by the German **Chief of Staff** Helmuth von Moltke. During August 1914, German troops fought their way across Belgium, encountering serious resistance from the Belgian army that slowed their progress long enough for the French and British to prepare their defences. By 20 August, the German troops had captured Brussels. Meanwhile, the French army was attacking along the French-German border and in southern Belgium. This series of clashes between the French and German armies became known as the Battle of the Frontiers.

THE END OF THE SCHLIEFFEN PLAN

The British government sent an army, called the British Expeditionary Force (BEF), to France in early August. British troops first saw action alongside the French army at the Battle of Mons (23 August). This battle held up the German advance, but it ended with an **Allied** (French and British) retreat as the German army pushed onwards. At this point, under Moltke's leadership, the Schlieffen Plan began to unravel. The speed of advance in the plan was a weakness. In many cases, supplies could not keep up with the movement of the troops. German soldiers, who had been almost continuously marching and fighting for several weeks, were becoming exhausted. Crucially, Moltke also decided to divert several divisions from the fighting in Belgium to help stop a Russian attack on the Eastern Front in East Prussia.

On 28 August, Kaiser Wilhelm II ordered the German army to begin its advance on Paris.[9] The city emptied as its citizens fled and the French government moved to Bordeaux. The German army advanced into the valley of the River Marne, north of Paris. The Battle of the Marne (6–10 September) was the turning point for the Germans. Unable to withstand Allied attacks, the German army retreated about 65 kilometres (40 miles), finally digging a defensive line along the River Aisne. Broken by the failure of the Schlieffen Plan, Moltke was replaced by a new German chief of staff, Erich von Falkenhayn.

The British army

Before World War I, the British regular army was tiny compared to those of its European neighbours. Many regular soldiers were posted around the world, policing the colonies of the British Empire. In the years leading up to 1914, a small extra force of six infantry **divisions** was trained and equipped to form the British Expeditionary Force (BEF) of just over 700,000. When war was declared, four of these divisions were sent to northern France to fight alongside the French army. At the same time, regular soldiers were recalled from their foreign posts. Lord Kitchener began his "call to arms" on 11 August 1914 to enlist volunteers for the army (see page 17). In late 1914 and early 1915, the army was also expanded by the arrival of troops from Britain's colonies, including Indians (see page 36–37), Canadians, Australians, and New Zealanders.[10]

THE FIRST BATTLE OF YPRES

During September 1914, attacks by the Allies on the German positions along the River Aisne proved fruitless. Attention turned instead to the area of land between the Aisne and the English Channel. Both sides tried to outmanouevre each other in a so-called "race to the sea", with the Germans trying to cut off the BEF from the Channel ports. The First Battle of Ypres, fought in October and November 1914, ended this phase of the fighting. Both the Germans and the Allies sustained heavy losses. By the end of the First Battle of Ypres, nearly all of the original members of the BEF had been killed.[11]

With winter setting in, the two sides fought themselves to a standstill. By the end of 1914, both the Allies and the Germans had dug themselves into lines of defensive trench systems, known as the Western Front, that stretched from the English Channel to the border with Switzerland. The war of movement had ended, and one of **attrition** had begun.

 These Belgian troops are taking up their position along the bank of a canal during the First Battle of Ypres, 1914.

ENTHUSIASM FOR THE WAR?

The declarations of war were greeted with outpourings of patriotism around Europe. Crowds gathered in London and other European cities as "war fever" took hold. In Britain, a speech by the foreign secretary, Sir Edward Grey, that justified British involvement in the war was greeted enthusiastically by members of Parliament. The *Morning Post* of 4 August reported: "Members rose from their seats, cheered and cheered again, and wildly waved hats and handkerchiefs."[12] In an address to Parliament on 6 August 1914, the prime minister, Herbert Asquith, stressed the moral basis for declaring war: "I do not believe any nation ever entered into a great controversy ... with a clearer conscience and a stronger conviction that it is fighting, not for aggression, not for the maintenance even of its own selfish interest, but ... in defence of principles the maintenance of which is vital to the civilization of the world."[13]

PROTEST AND PROPAGANDA

Yet enthusiasm for the war was not universal. Even some politicians who publicly backed the war, privately expressed their doubts. Sir Edward Grey famously remarked to a friend on the outbreak of war that "The lamps are going out all over Europe; we shall not see them lit again in our lifetime".[14] Others were open in their opposition to war. These included members of the anti-war group, the Union of Democratic Control,[15] and left-wing organizations, such as the Independent Labour Party.[16] In a letter to the magazine *The Nation* on 15 August, the British philosopher and **pacifist** Bertrand Russell wrote: "Against the vast majority of my countrymen ... in the name of humanity and civilization, I protest against our share in the destruction of Germany..."[17]

The British government realized the need to ensure public support for its actions. The newspapers were largely supportive of the war effort. Nevertheless, the government quickly introduced the Defence of the Realm Act (DORA) to impose press **censorship** (see page 54 for more about DORA). It also set up the War **Propaganda** Bureau to try to influence public opinion both at home and abroad. Recruits to this Bureau were influential and well-known writers including Thomas Hardy, H.G. Wells, Robert Bridges, Sir Arthur Conan Doyle, and J.M. Barrie.[18] As part of his work for the Bureau, H.G. Wells published a book called *The War That Will End War*. As the title suggests, Wells justified this war by arguing that it would put an end to future wars: "...war is mortal conflict. We have now either to destroy or be destroyed. We have not sought this reckoning, we have done our utmost to avoid it; but now that it has been forced upon us it is imperative that it should be a thorough reckoning."[19]

The need for volunteers

Many people believed that the war would be "over by Christmas". The Minister for War, Lord Kitchener, thought differently. In August 1914, he launched a campaign, "Your Country Needs You", to recruit thousands of volunteers for the British army. "Who's Absent? Is It YOU?" and "Daddy, What did YOU do in the Great War?" were some of the poster slogans used to attract recruits.[20] The campaign was very successful – the first 100,000 men were enlisted in the space of two weeks.[21] Before **conscription** was introduced in 1916, almost 2.5 million men had volunteered to serve in the British army.[22]

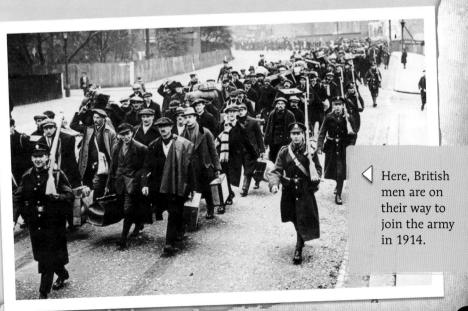

◁ Here, British men are on their way to join the army in 1914.

THE DARDANELLES AND GALLIPOLI

In October 1914, the Ottoman Empire (Turkey) had entered the war on the side of the **Central Powers** (Germany and Austria-Hungary).[1] In Britain, the First Lord of the Admiralty, Winston Churchill, believed that the time was right for an attack on the Ottoman Empire. The Dardanelles Strait links the Aegean Sea with the Sea of Marmara, providing a route to the Black Sea and Russian ports. Churchill wanted to seize control of this important supply route, and to help the Russians by diverting Turkish troops away from battles in the east.[2] He also hoped that the prestige of a victory would persuade countries such as Bulgaria to enter the war on the side of the Allies. From February 1915 until January 1916, the Allies undertook a campaign to take control of the Dardanelles Strait and western Turkey.[3]

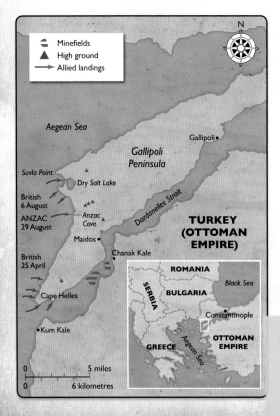

A naval attack was launched in February 1915, but after losing three battleships, the navy retreated in March. In April, Allied ground troops began an attack on the Gallipoli Peninsula. They included some British, French, and Indian, but mostly Anzac (Australian and New Zealand) troops. Preparations for the landings at Cape Helles

The Gallipoli Peninsula was the scene of fierce fighting in 1915.

and Ari Burnu (renamed Anzac Cove) were badly managed, and the Allied troops encountered fierce resistance from defending Turkish soldiers. There were many casualties, and the Allied troops were unable to move beyond the **beachheads** on which they had landed. New landings at Suvla Bay on the west coast in August led to more fierce fighting and heavy casualties, but no breakthrough.

RESIGNATION AND EVACUATION

In November 1915, Churchill resigned from the government. After a visit by Lord Kitchener to the peninsula, the decision was taken to evacuate all Allied troops. This took place over three weeks in December 1915 and January 1916 with remarkably few casualties. Overall, however, the campaign had been a costly failure. It had taken 480,000 soldiers away from the fighting on the Western Front, with 252,000 of these men being injured or killed. The Anzac troops suffered particularly badly – nearly 34,000 were injured or killed.[4] Although the campaign had diverted Turkish troops who would otherwise have been fighting elsewhere, it had failed to open up a supply route to Russia. It also helped to convince Bulgaria to join with the Central Powers rather than the Allies.[5]

BIOGRAPHY

Winston Churchill 1874–1965

BORN: Blenheim Palace, Oxfordshire

ROLE: He was a statesman and writer. In his early life he served in the army as a soldier and a journalist in India and Africa. He was elected to Parliament in 1900. During World War I he was First Lord of the Admiralty (1911–1915), returning to active service with the army in France after his resignation over Gallipoli. In 1917 he was appointed as Minister of **Munitions** and oversaw the development of the tank. During World War II, he was again First Lord of the Admiralty, and then Prime Minister (1940–1945). He was knighted in 1953.

DID YOU KNOW? Churchill won the Nobel Prize for Literature in 1953, "for his mastery of historical and biographical description as well as for brilliant oratory in defending exalted human values".

ALBERT JACKA

"He was a soldier with both physical and moral courage of the highest order... He hated the necessity of war, but felt it to be a necessity; and he would see his job through." Rev. F.W. Rolland, MC, MAMufti, 1 January 1937

One of the most famous of the Anzac troops who fought at Gallipoli was Albert Jacka. He joined up in September 1914, and spent two months training in Egypt before landing at Anzac Cove on 26 April 1915. Jacka and the rest of the Anzac troops then dug themselves into defensive trenches above the beach as best they could. On 19 May, the Turkish defenders launched an attack that was designed to drive the invaders back towards the sea. However, Anzac observers had been watching Turkish preparations for the attack. When it started, the Anzac soldiers were ready for it. As wave after wave of Turks came towards the Anzac defences, they were cut down by gunfire.

Anzac Day

In both Australia and New Zealand, the first day of the Gallipoli landings, 25 April, is commemorated every year as "Anzac Day". On this day, Australians and New Zealanders now remember all their countrymen and women who have died serving their country.[6] Despite the military failure, the Gallipoli campaign left behind a powerful legacy. The courage and endurance of the Anzac troops gave a new sense of independence and pride, and helped to foster a sense of national identity in both countries.[7]

In one part of the Anzac trench, however, the Turks did break through. This trench was guarded at one end by Lance Corporal Jacka. After firing warning shots for several minutes while reinforcements arrived, Jacka and three others attempted an attack on the Turks. The other Anzac soldiers were immediately hit and injured. Jacka quickly retreated to devise a new plan. Two bombs were thrown to create a diversion. In the noise and confusion, Jacka ran round a back way to the occupied trench, jumped in, and single-handedly killed several Turkish soldiers.[8]

HERO IN THE EAST AND THE WEST

For his bravery, Jacka was awarded the Victoria Cross – the highest military honour awarded to British and Commonwealth soldiers. He was the first Australian to receive this military honour in World War I. As such, he also received some money and a gold watch that had been promised by an Australian businessman to the first winner of the medal. He became an instant hero in Australia. His image was used on recruiting posters, and from that time his exploits were widely reported in the Australian newspapers.[9] After Gallipoli, he was sent to the Western Front. Once again, his bravery was outstanding. In one incident at Pozières, he led a small group of men to save 40 Australian soldiers who were being taken prisoner. During this exchange, Jacka was seriously wounded and was sent to hospital in London. In September 1915, some newspapers reported that he had died, but the reports were untrue. For his actions in Pozières, he was awarded another high-level military honour, the Military Cross.

Jacka survived further action in France, and eventually returned to Australia in 1919. He died in 1932. His funeral was attended by thousands of ex-Anzac troops.[10]

He kept his Pledge

JACKA

YOU BUY PEACE BONDS

▷ As well as being used for recruitment posters, Albert Jacka's heroic image was also used on posters urging the public to invest its money in the war effort.

THE EASTERN FRONT

Just like Germany and France, Russia had a battle plan drawn up well before war broke out in 1914. "Plan 19" was devised by General Yuri Danilov in 1910, and it was based – correctly, as it turned out – on the belief that Germany would attack France before it attacked Russia. In response, Danilov planned a **pincer** movement on East Prussia, the easternmost province of the German Empire.[1] The plan was revised in 1912 because of fears of the threat from Austria-Hungary. In the event, two Russian armies were sent into action in East Prussia, while two remained in Russia to defend against any attack from Austria-Hungary.[2]

RUSSIAN DEFEATS

The 1st and 2nd Russian armies, commanded by General Paul von Rennenkampf and General Alexander Samsonov, marched into East Prussia in August 1914. Their forces outnumbered those of the opposing German forces by two to one.[3] The plan was for the two armies to meet and combine, pushing the Germans back. Rennenkampf's 1st army had initial victories at Stalluponen (17 August) and Gumbinnen (20 August). At this point,

The Russian Army

With a huge population (see page 11), Russia had large reserves of manpower to call upon for its army. But Russia's vast size meant that the logistics of moving soldiers and equipment from one place to another was always a problem. The Germans had based the Schlieffen Plan on a calculation that the Russian army would take six weeks to mobilize.[4] In fact, the construction of new railways in Russia had considerably cut down the time needed for mobilization.[5] In 1904–05, Russia's navy and Imperial Army had suffered a humiliating defeat in a war with Japan[6] (see pages 26–27). In the wake of this defeat, attempts were made to reorganize and reform the army. But many of the Russian generals found it difficult to modernize. For example, despite the development of powerful guns that could easily wipe out both horses and riders, the Russian Imperial Army continued to rely heavily on its **cavalry** in battle.[7]

This map shows the Eastern Front from 1914 to 1918. The battles on this front were fought across a huge area of Europe.

Map legend:
- German or Austrian advances
- Russian advances
- Limits of Russian advances 1914–15
- Limits of German and Austrian advances 1915–16
- Brusilov Offensive 1916
- German gains September 1917
- German or Austrian gains until 3 March 1918

0   200 miles

0   300 kilometres

**Map labels:** FINLAND, St Petersburg, Riga, Baltic Sea, Königsberg, Danzig, East Prussia, Tannenberg, Masurian Lakes, GERMANY, Warsaw, Brest-Litovsk, Minsk, Pripet Marshes, RUSSIA, Cracow, Galicia, Budapest, AUSTRIA-HUNGARY, Odessa, Belgrade, ROMANIA, Black Sea

Rennenkampf stopped his army's advance in order to regroup. The Germans, meanwhile, were surrounding Samsonov's 2nd army. Unaware of the danger, Samsonov's situation was made worse when the Germans intercepted uncoded messages that made it clear that his army would not receive support from Rennenkampf's forces.[8] In the Battle of Tannenberg, the 2nd army was crushed by the Germans. Out of an army of 150,000 men, only about 10,000 escaped.[9] The rest were killed or taken prisoner. Samsonov shot himself, unable to face the consequences of the disaster.

The German commander, Paul von Hindenburg, now turned his attention to the Russian 1st army. At the First Battle of the Masurian Lakes, Rennenkampf was forced to retreat. By 13 September, he had withdrawn all his troops from East Prussia. He did, however, mount a **counter-attack** that forced the German army back once again and reclaimed much of the ground Russia had lost in the previous battle.[10]

ATTACKS IN GALICIA

While Russia's 1st and 2nd armies were busy in East Prussia, its 3rd and 8th armies moved into Galicia, the northernmost province of Austria-Hungary. The Russians made rapid progress through Galicia in the autumn of 1914. Austria-Hungary had, meanwhile, invaded Russian Poland.[11] By late in the year, the army of Austria-Hungary, now backed up by German forces, had established a defensive line along the Carpathian Mountains.

Poison gas

On 31 January 1915, a German attack on the Russian army was launched at Bolimov in Poland. This attack was designed to draw Russian attention away from the Masurian Lakes region further north. The Battle of Bolimov is mainly remembered today because it saw the first use of poison gas in World War I. The Germans fired shells containing a type of **tear gas**. The experiment failed, as the gas, which was stored as a liquid, could not **vaporize** in the freezing conditions and fell harmlessly to the ground.[14]

SECOND BATTLE OF THE MASURIAN LAKES

Further north, the Second Battle of the Masurian Lakes was fought in the bitterly cold winter of February 1915, between the Russian and German armies. The battle was an attempt by Paul von Hindenburg to bring to an end the fighting on the Eastern Front. The German Chief of Staff, Erich von Falkenhayn, was reluctant to divert troops from the fighting on the Western Front, but he was won over.[12] The Russians were encircled by the German army, and were forced to retreat and flee. Thousands were taken prisoner. Although the battle did not bring a conclusive end to fighting on the Eastern Front, it did finally drive the Russians from East Prussia and end the threat there.[13]

RETREAT AND ATTACK

Throughout the spring and summer of 1915, the Russian army was gradually pushed back by a series of Austro-German **offensives**. By September 1915, the "Great Retreat" was over. Russia had surrendered all of its territories in Poland. However, the retreat had been a skilful one – weapons and other equipment had been dismantled and transported to safe areas, and a large part of the Russian army was still intact.[15]

Most fighting stopped over the winter, but 1916 saw another major offensive on the Eastern Front, this time from the Russians. The Brusilov Offensive, named after General Alexei Brusilov, began on 4 June 1916 along a front that extended 320 kilometres (200 miles) from Lutsk in the north to the border with Romania in the south. The attack took the Austrian army by surprise. Within a month the Russians had made considerable advances and had taken 350,000 Austrian prisoners. More attacks followed into October. Once again, the Central Powers were forced to move troops from the Western Front to fight the Russians. The Brusilov Offensive crippled the Austrian army, but the Russians suffered huge numbers of casualties, too – an estimated 1 million men dead, wounded, or taken prisoner. An exhausted army, and famine and riots at home, set the scene for the dramatic events of 1917 in Russia – the Russian Revolution.[16]

These Russian prisoners of war are being escorted by German guards.

TSAR NICHOLAS II

Nikolai Aleksandrovich Romanov was born near St Petersburg, on 18 May 1868. He was the eldest son of Tsar Alexander III. He succeeded to the throne in 1894 and in the same year he married Princess Alexandra of Hesse-Darmstadt (a duchy in Germany). Nicholas was devoted to his wife, and her influence over him was to play a large part in the events that followed.

As tsar, Nicholas was the ruler of a huge empire that stretched from central Europe in the west to the Pacific Ocean in the east. He believed that he derived his authority to rule from God, and these **autocratic** views were strongly reinforced by Alexandra. When, early on in his reign, representatives from various local assemblies asked him for reforms to the government he dismissed their petitions as "senseless dreams".

CONFLICT WITH JAPAN

Nicholas was keen to expand Russian influence in the Far East, particularly in Manchuria (modern-day northeast China) and Korea. This led Russia into conflict with Japan. In 1904, the Japanese attacked the Russian fleet in Port Arthur, in the Yellow Sea. The war

This family portrait shows Tsar Nicholas II with his wife, Alexandra, and his five children.

that followed was a disaster for Russia, as its troops were forced to retreat through Manchuria, and its Baltic Fleet was destroyed by the Japanese at the Battle of Tsushima. The war caused increasing unrest in Russia. In January 1905, the army opened fire on demonstrators in St Petersburg. Nicholas was unwilling to make any compromises, but was eventually forced to accept the creation of a representative assembly, the Duma.

Nicholas and Alexandra had four daughters and one son, Alexei, the heir to the throne. Alexei suffered from haemophilia, a disease that prevented his blood from clotting. At the time, there was no effective medical treatment for the disease. In desperation Alexandra turned increasingly to a mystic monk, Grigori Rasputin, for help. Rasputin gained great power over both Alexandra and Nicholas. He was eventually murdered in 1916.

After the disastrous campaigns of 1915, Nicholas decided against all advice to take on the command of the Russian armies himself. This move meant that every military failure became associated with him personally. Even worse, with Nicholas away from St Petersburg for much of the time, responsibility for government passed to Alexandra, who was by now firmly under the influence of Rasputin.

Food shortages, poverty, and the massive casualties of war led to increasing unrest. In March 1917, having lost the support of the government and the army, Nicholas was forced to **abdicate**. He and his family were executed in July 1918.

Nicky to Willy

This is one of the letters written by Nicholas (Nicky) to his cousin Kaiser Wilhelm II of Germany to try to avert the outbreak of war:[17]

Peter's Court, Palace,
1 August 1914

Sa Majesté l'Empereur Berlin,
I received your telegram. Understand you are obliged to mobilize but wish to have the same guarantee from you as I gave you, that these measures do not mean war and that we shall continue negotiating for the benefit of our countries and universal peace dear to all our hearts. Our long proved friendship must succeed, with God's help, in avoiding bloodshed. Anxiously, full of confidence await your answer.

Nicky

THE WAR AT SEA

The pre-war race to build up the British and German navies was won by the British, who entered the war with a larger and better-equipped navy (see table below). Neither country wanted a direct confrontation between the two fleets, as neither wanted to lose ships in battle. Instead, the Germans planned to use mines and submarine attacks to challenge British supremacy at sea. The main aims of the British navy were to protect vital trade routes into Britain, and to prevent supplies reaching Germany by enforcing a **blockade** of the North Sea.[1]

Naval strengths in 1914[2]

	Britain	Germany
Dreadnoughts	24	13
Battle cruisers	8	5
Light cruisers	35	33
Submarines	44	38

Here, a ship takes a hit during the Battle of Heligoland.

Room 40

By three extraordinary pieces of luck, the British intelligence services were able to intercept and decode German naval communications throughout the war. In August 1914, a German light cruiser, the *Magdeburg*, ran aground off the Russian coast. A naval code book retrieved from the ship was sent to the Admiralty in London, where code-breakers set to work in an office that became known as "Room 40". In October, another German code book was captured by the Australian navy and sent to Room 40. A short time after, a third code book was pulled up in the fishing nets of a British trawler. It, too, was passed on to the Admiralty. Using all this information, the British intelligence services were frequently able to warn the navy about German plans.[3]

NORTH SEA BATTLES

The first naval engagement of the war took place on 28 August 1914 at Heligoland Bight.[4] In misty conditions, the British navy succeeded in sinking three German light cruisers and a destroyer.[5] In retaliation, in November and again in December, the German fleet bombarded the North Sea ports of Yarmouth, Scarborough, Hartlepool, and Whitby. Despite intelligence from Room 40 (see panel above), the British navy did not manage to intercept the German fleet. The British had more success in January 1915, at the battle of Dogger Bank. Warned once again by Room 40, cruisers of the British fleet sank the German cruiser *Blücher* and badly damaged another ship. This action was enough for Kaiser Wilhelm II to order the German fleet to remain in its home bases.[6]

With their surface fleet confined to port, the Germans concentrated on other means of attack – by **mines** and by submarines. They had already had some notable successes. On 22 September, **torpedoes** fired from a German U-boat (*Unterseeboot* is German for "submarine") had sunk three British cruisers, and on 27 October a German mine sunk the British battleship *Audacious*.[7] In February 1915, Germany declared unrestricted submarine warfare. This meant that German U-boats would attack merchant shipping without warning (see page 33). In retaliation, Britain stepped up the blockade of Germany, banning neutral countries, such as the USA, from trading with Germany.

THE *LUSITANIA*

On 1 May 1915, a passenger liner, the *Lusitania*, left New York with more than 1,200 passengers and 700 crew onboard. Alongside the advertisement for the voyage was a notice from the German Embassy which warned passengers that "vessels flying the flag of Great Britain, or any of her allies, are liable to destruction ... and that travellers sailing in the war zone on ships of Great Britain or her allies do so at their own risk".[8] On 7 May, as the ship entered the Irish Channel, a German U-boat torpedoed it. The liner sank and 1,201 people drowned, including 128 US citizens.[9] The sinking caused outrage, particularly in the United States. In August another liner, the *Arabic*, was sunk, again with the loss of American lives. In September 1915, in fear of provoking the United States any further, Germany suspended all of its submarine activity in British waters.[10]

WHEN YOU FIRE REMEMBER THIS

ENLIST IN THE NAVY

THE BATTLE OF JUTLAND

In January 1916, Admiral Reinhard Scheer took over the command of the German navy. He and many of the captains of the German fleet found it difficult to justify the inactivity of the navy, particularly when the German army were sustaining huge casualties on the battlefields of the Western Front.[11] Scheer decided to take his fleet

◁ The outrage over the sinking of the *Lusitania* was used to stir up patriotic feelings in this US propaganda poster.

out into the North Sea once again, in search of action. This decision resulted in the biggest naval battle of World War I, the Battle of Jutland. Once again, the British were helped by intelligence from Room 40 which gave them advance notice of the German plan of battle. This huge battle, fought on 31 May, ended indecisively. The British fleet lost several major ships, and the German fleet escaped back to its home ports, but the British remained in control of the North Sea.[12] Again, the German fleet was confined to the safety of its home ports.

SUBMARINE ATTACKS

The second half of 1916 was a time of heated debate in the German high command over whether to reintroduce unrestricted submarine warfare. The stakes were high – some thought that an all-out attack on merchant shipping would quickly bring Britain to the brink of starvation, others believed that such attacks would force the USA to enter the war. Eventually, on 1 February 1917, a campaign of unrestricted submarine warfare was declared. The Germans calculated that the blockade could force Britain to the negotiating table before the USA could mobilize. Their gamble nearly paid off. From February to April 1917, U-boats sank more than 500 merchant ships.[13] Only when the Allies introduced a **convoy** system (see panel below) did the rate of loss slow down. The USA duly declared war in April 1917 (see page 48).

Convoys

The solution to U-boat attacks was for merchant ships to sail in armed convoys. Although there was some initial opposition to this plan, it was first tried out in May 1917. Instead of sailing independently, merchant ships were grouped together and surrounded by a protective ring of naval ships. From May onwards, regular convoys meant that the number of sinkings declined rapidly. As one U-boat commander remarked: "The oceans at once became bare and empty."[14]

U-BOATS

PRIZE RULES

The sinking of three British cruisers early on in the war (see page 29) demonstrated how dangerous U-boats were against warships. But as weapons to enforce a blockade, U-boats were not at first considered very effective. This was because both the German and British navies operated under "prize rules", an agreement which stated that passenger ships could not be attacked, and that if a merchant ship was attacked, the crew had to be taken off to safety before it was sunk.[15] Attacks under prize rules were completely impractical for U-boats. The submarines were too small to take on prisoners, and it was very risky for them to come to the surface to attack a merchant ship, which might very well try to ram them.

Unrestricted submarine warfare, first declared by the Germans in February 1915, ignored the prize rules. Merchant ships and passenger liners suspected of carrying war supplies were sunk without warning. It was a dangerous tactic as it risked bringing powerful neutral countries such as the USA into the war. But in 1917, unrestricted submarine warfare very nearly succeeded in crippling Britain.

▽ German U-boats, such as the one below, could inflict terrible damage on enemy warships if the German navy ignored the prize rules.

UP CLOSE

Q-SHIPS

The British came up with various counter-measures against the U-boat threat including **decoy** ships, known as Q-ships. These were merchant ships fitted out with hidden guns. They carried cargoes of wood and cork that made them almost unsinkable by torpedo. Their aim was to lure the U-boat to the surface, then to drop the panels that concealed the guns and open fire.[16] The first Q-ship to sink a U-boat was HMS *Prince Charles* on 24 July 1915. But the German U-boat commanders soon grew wary of these decoys. British Q-ships were responsible for the sinking of 14 U-boats, and damaging another 60. Out of around 200 Q-ships, 27 were lost in action.[17]

BIOGRAPHY

Lothar von Arnauld de la Perière 1886–1941

BORN: Posen (Poznan), Prussia (now part of Poland)

ROLE: U-boat captain from 1915 to 1918.

DID YOU KNOW? He was the most successful U-boat captain of World War I. He sank 194 ships, all according to prize rules. He wrote of his wartime experiences: "My record cruise was quite tame and dull. We stopped the vessels. The crews boarded the lifeboats. We inspected the ships' documents, told the crews how they could reach the next port, and then sank the stopped prize."[18]

The commander's story

This account by the commander of a U-boat describes the view through his periscope as a torpedo is launched and hits a merchant ship in 1916:

"I saw that the bubble-track of the torpedo had been discovered on the bridge of the steamer ... Then a frightful explosion followed, and we were all thrown against one another by the concussion ... All her [the merchant ship's] decks were visible to me. From all the hatchways a storming, despairing mass of men were fighting their way on deck, grimy stokers, officers, soldiers, groom, cooks. They all rushed, ran, screamed for boats, tore and thrust one another from the ladders leading down to them, fought for the lifebelts, and jostled one another on the sloping deck..."[19]

33

THE WESTERN FRONT

By the end of 1914, the Allies and the Central Powers had fought themselves to a standstill on the Western Front. The Germans had failed to achieve the swift victory in the West dictated by the Schlieffen Plan, and they now adopted a policy of defence. They dug deep and well-constructed trench systems, and settled down to defend the territory they had gained during the past few months. The German commander, Erich von Falkenhayn, knew that he needed to concentrate a large number of troops on the Eastern Front, where the Germans were trying to knock the Russians out of the war.

ON THE OFFENSIVE

The French, however, took a very different view of the situation. The land occupied by the Germans contained much of France's natural reserves of coal and iron, and most of its manufacturing industries.[1] For the French it was also a matter of national pride to win back these provinces. The French commander, General Joseph Joffre, was determined to mount attacks on areas of the German front line that seemed vulnerable. He was backed by the British, who were continuing to send large numbers of troops to France, including the first of Kitchener's "New Armies" (see page 14). The Allies believed that they could break through the German line at certain vulnerable points. Once the German defences had been penetrated, the Allies' plan was to attack the railway lines that kept the German troops supplied with food, equipment, and ammunition.[2]

The French army had launched an offensive in Champagne in December 1914, but this was called off in March after heavy rain had flooded the trenches and made any advance impossible. There were 90,000 French casualties but no gain in territory. The first major offensive of 1915 was at Neuve Chapelle in March. The attack was preceded by a massive **bombardment** of enemy lines which took the Germans completely by surprise. The British troops advanced and made ground quickly as the Germans retreated. But communications between the front line troops and their commanders, about 8 kilometres (5 miles) away, were very slow. By the time new orders arrived, the Germans had taken the opportunity to bring in reinforcements. In this offensive, which lasted three days, there were 11,200 Allied casualties (7,000 British, 4,200 Indian).[3] Once again, there was no significant gain in territory.

Gas attack!

The Germans first used gas as a weapon unsuccessfully on the Eastern Front (see page 24). On 22 April, they tried it again at the Second Battle of Ypres. Around 6,000 canisters of chlorine gas were released, sending a dense greenish-yellow cloud towards the Allied trenches. This time the poison gas did its work. Many of the Allied French and Algerian soldiers died in their trenches; some soldiers were taken prisoner, while others fled, blinded and choking. A 7-kilometre (4-mile) gap was left in the Allied front line, but the Germans were so surprised by the success of the attack that they failed to take full advantage of this breakthrough.[4]

▽ These British machine gunners are wearing gas masks to protect themselves from a gas attack.

INDIAN TROOPS ON THE WESTERN FRONT

In 1914, Britain looked to its colonies around the world to provide some of the manpower so desperately needed for fighting the war. India had a large and well-trained army. Two Indian infantry divisions totalling around 44,000 men arrived in Marseilles, in southern France, in late September and October 1914. Many of these troops were quickly moved north into position to fight in the battles around Ypres (see page 15).

SUFFERING IN THE COLD

The Indian troops had arrived in France dressed in light khaki drill uniforms, suitable for the hot climate they had come from rather than the cold, wet climate of Belgium and northern France.[5] For them, the cold was a real enemy. As winter set in, many succumbed to frostbite, as well as illnesses such as influenza and pneumonia. They were eventually kitted out with thicker, warmer uniforms. The plight of the Indian troops resulted in great sympathy from well-wishers in Britain who sent gifts of knitted scarves and other items to keep the soldiers warm.[6]

In December 1914, the trenches became so wet and clogged with mud that an order was given for the Indian soldiers to retreat and regroup. Already over 2,000 of their number had been killed.[7] The Indian troops next saw action in March 1915 at Neuve Chapelle (see page 34), where another 4,200 Indian soldiers died in the space of three days. Then, during an offensive near Ypres in April, there were many more casualties as a result of a German gas attack. One Indian soldier wrote in a letter home: "This is not war; it is the ending of the world."[8] The massive casualties suffered by the Indian divisions, combined with the cold, led to a rapid decline in morale. The decision was taken to withdraw the Indian troops from the Western Front, except for two cavalry (mounted) brigades. The Indian cavalry continued to fight bravely on the Western Front until 1918. The infantry, meanwhile, were sent to fight in the warmer climate of Egypt.

INDIAN LABOUR CORPS

As well as the Indian soldiers who fought on the Western Front, around 21,000 Indians also worked in the Labour Corps. This was the organization that provided essential services to the army, for example cooking, laundry, moving supplies and stores, burying the dead, unloading ships and trains, and repairing roads and railways.[9] Many of the Labour Corps worked far behind the front lines, but the Indian labourers were often used for more dangerous work close to the action, such as building fortifications or moving ammunition. Today, the names of members of the Indian Labour Corps who died on the Western Front are found alongside those of Indian soldiers in many of the military cemeteries in northern France.

The Royal Pavilion

Many Indian soldiers who were injured in action on the Western Front were taken to Britain for treatment. Some were taken to the Royal Pavilion in Brighton, a late 18th-century palace built in an exotic Indian style for the Prince Regent (later King George IV). During World War I, the pavilion was turned into a military hospital specifically for the Indian soldiers, with 742 beds.[10]

Here, soldiers of the Indian army are pictured in France with their bicycles.

Map labels:
- 0 — 50 miles
- 0 — 50 kilometres
- N
- North Sea
- HOLLAND
- River Rhine
- Zeebrugge
- Ostend
- •Antwerp
- BELGIUM
- Cologne•
- Passchendaele
- July 1917
- June 1917 — •Ypres
- •Brussels
- •Aix-la-Chapelle
- Messines
- March 1915 — •Neuve Chapelle
- April 1918
- Sept 1915 — •Loos
- River Sambre
- GERMANY
- April 1917 — Vimy Ridge
- Arras •
- April 1917
- •Cambrai
- Le Cateau
- July 1916 — •Albert
- Amiens• March 1918
- July 1915
- •Sedan
- LUXEMBOURG
- April 1917 — May 1918
- Soissons•
- April 1917
- Feb 1916
- Feb 1916
- Reims• Verdun•
- •Metz
- FRANCE
- April 1917
- •St Mihiel
- Paris•
- Sept 1918
- •Nancy
- River Seine

Legend:
- → Dates of major offensives
- ∙∙∙∙∙ Approximate front at end of 1914
- — Front on 11 November 1918

△ This map shows the Western Front from 1914 to 1918. Troops fought to and fro across the same areas of land for four years.

VERDUN

At the beginning of 1916, in an attempt to break the French army, the Germans launched a major attack on the French fortress of Verdun. General von Falkenhayn reasoned that if the Germans could inflict massive casualties, "the forces of France would bleed to death".[11] A knock-out blow to the French could, he thought, also bring Britain to its knees.[12] Falkenhayn chose Verdun for the attack because he knew that the fortress was an important status symbol for the French. He counted on the fact that they would defend it fiercely.

Falkenhayn's shrewd calculation was correct. The German assault on Verdun began on 21 February. Three days later, the Germans had captured the stronghold of Fort Douaumont, and Verdun looked extremely vulnerable. At that point a new commander, Philippe Pétain, was put in charge of French operations at Verdun. He was determined not to lose the fort. He sent a message to the commander of the troops around Verdun: "I have taken command. Tell your troops. Hold fast."[13] This was exactly what Falkenhayn wanted. Pétain sent in reinforcements along the only supply route to the fort, which came to be known as "*la voie sacrée*" (the sacred way). The fighting dragged on for months, with heavy casualties on both the French and German sides. By the end of June, a total of more than 200,000 men (on both sides) had been killed and injured in the fighting at Verdun.

THE SOMME

In July 1916, attention switched away from Verdun to another part of the Western Front. The Allies had been planning an offensive in the region of the Somme since the beginning of 1916. However, the timing of the attack was brought forward to relieve French forces at Verdun. The British commander in charge of the offensive was Douglas Haig.

BIOGRAPHY

Sir Douglas Haig 1861–1928

BORN: Edinburgh, Scotland

ROLE: Commander-in-Chief of the BEF 1915–1918. He remains a controversial figure because of the huge numbers of casualties sustained under his command at the Battle of the Somme (1916) and at the Third Battle of Ypres (1917, also called Passchendaele). His policy of attrition has been summarized as "kill more Germans".

DID YOU KNOW? After the war, Haig helped to establish the Royal British Legion (an organization dedicated to the care of those who had suffered as a result of service in the armed forces in World War I) and devoted his life to the welfare of soldiers who had served during the war.[14]

The German trenches along the Somme were deep and well-defended. On 24 June the Allies began a week-long bombing of the German front lines. The shelling was meant to empty the German lines in preparation for a massive Allied attack. Many Germans survived by retreating to their fortifications. On 1 July, thousands of Allied troops moved in waves towards the German lines. They expected little or no opposition. In fact, they were met by lethal machine gun fire from the well-protected German positions. Of the 100,000 British soldiers who attacked that day, 20,000 died and another 40,000 were wounded. Despite the appalling loss of life, the battle on the Somme continued until 19 November.[15]

ATTACK AND DEFENCE

In December 1916, General Robert Nivelle became commander of the French forces. Nivelle had taken over from Pétain at Verdun, and was responsible for the eventual recapture of the fort. He now planned a new Allied offensive for 1917 to squeeze the Germans between two attacks in Champagne and Arras. He predicted that the offensive would achieve success within two days.[16] However, as a result of lapses in security, Nivelle's plans became known to the Germans.[17]

In fact, the German commanders Paul von Hindenburg and Erich von Ludendorff already had plans of their own. During autumn 1916, the Germans had been building a series of linked fortifications up to 48 kilometres (30 miles) behind their own front line. This fortified line was called the Siegfried Line by the Germans, but became known to the Allies as the Hindenburg Line (after Paul von Hindenburg). During the spring of 1917, the Germans gradually began to move back to the Hindenburg Line. As they retreated they adopted a "scorched earth" policy – they destroyed everything that might possibly be of use to the Allies. They also laid mines and booby traps to make the area as dangerous as possible for attacking troops. The Hindenburg Line was considerably shorter than the old German front line, and required fewer soldiers to defend it, freeing up troops to go to the Eastern Front.

THE NIVELLE OFFENSIVE

Despite the German retreat, Nivelle decided to press on with his offensive. On 9 April, the Battle of Arras started the offensive well, with Canadian troops capturing Vimy Ridge. But the Germans were forewarned and well-prepared for the French attack along an 80-kilometre (50-mile) front further south in Aisne. In the massacre that followed, the French suffered 187,000 casualties.[18] In the aftermath, morale in the French army was so low that **mutinies** broke out. Amongst other things, the soldiers demanded better food and more **leave**. In May 1917, Nivelle was replaced by Pétain, who listened to the soldiers' grievances, and gradually restored order in the French army.

War poetry

The grim experience of life in the trenches on the Western Front inspired all sorts of writing, including poetry. Some of the writers were already poets before they went to fight, others turned to poetry as a much-needed means of expressing the fear and horrors of their experiences. In his poem, "Exposure", Wilfred Owen described freezing winter conditions in a front-line trench at night:

"Our brains ache, in the merciless iced east winds that knife us …
Wearied we keep awake because the night is silent …"[19]

△ Like Owen, Seigfried Sassoon (1886-1967) also fought in World War I and expressed his hatred of war through his poetry.

THE CHANGING NATURE OF WARFARE

The trenches of the Western Front were deep ditches. In wet or stony ground where it was difficult to dig deep, a trench often had a sheltering wall, or **parapet**, along the top of the side facing the enemy. The trenches nearest the enemy were known as the "front line" and the area in-between the two front lines was "**no man's land**". This varied in width from several kilometres in some places to just a few metres in others. Both sides fixed tangles and rolls of barbed wire in no man's land to act as barriers against attack.

The front line trenches were connected by communication trenches to reserve trenches further back. As the war progressed, these trench systems became increasingly complicated. The Germans, in particular, spent a great deal of time and energy building deep trench systems. Some trenches even had wooden bunks and electric light. With more emphasis on offensive tactics, the French and British were less inclined to invest so much effort into building trenches that they hoped not to occupy for long.

KEEP YOUR HEAD DOWN!

The trenches were busiest at night when, under the cover of darkness, troops moved in and out, fetched supplies, made forays into no man's land to repair and lay barbed wire, or to attempt to collect dead bodies for burial. During the day, movement around the trenches was often dangerous. Even the briefest glimpse over the parapet could result in a bullet through the head from a **sniper's** rifle. Other hazards included flooding and constant mud, lice, trench rats that could grow as big as cats, and "trench fever" caused by the unsanitary conditions.[1]

COMMUNICATIONS

One of the biggest difficulties experienced by both sides during the fighting on the Western Front was communications. All sorts of different methods were employed to relay information and commands, including human runners, signalling lamps, messenger-dogs, and carrier pigeons. Both the Germans and the Allies developed elaborate networks of field telephones. These were connected by wires that were buried beneath trenches or fixed to trench walls. One problem was that the wires were easily broken by **artillery** fire. Another was that as attacking soldiers moved forward, they went even further away from the nearest point of communication. Several offensives failed because commanders had no accurate information about what was actually happening on the ground, and because orders took too long to reach front-line troops.

Wireless

The photo below shows German troops operating a field telephone on the Western Front. Wireless radio sets were also used in World War I, but they were large, heavy, and cumbersome. This is an account by a young wireless operator describing the moment he is told that he will be going in to attack with the infantry at Arras in 1917:[2]

"The attack was to be made within the next few days, the infantry waves were to advance under cover of a formidable barrage, and each wave was to be provided with a wireless station. The Roclincourt station was to go over with the first infantry wave. The Roclincourt station! That was Hewitt and I and an officer! Four infantrymen were to assist us in carrying our weighty apparatus, the set, accumulators, dry cells, coils of wire, earth mats, ropes, and other details…"

WEAPONS

The soldiers on the Western Front were equipped with rifles. A sharp blade, called a **bayonet**, could be attached to the end of the rifle for hand-to-hand combat. Machine guns, which could fire continuous rounds of bullets, were a powerful defensive weapon. Although the early machine guns were cumbersome, requiring a team of four to six men to operate them, their effectiveness was demonstrated in battles such as the Somme, where thousands of attacking Allied troops were mown down by German machine gun fire. Lighter and faster guns were developed as the war progressed.[3] Bombs, **grenades**, **trench mortars**, and flamethrowers were also widely used by the opposing armies.

Behind the front line, the big guns – artillery – were used to bombard the enemy with shells. As the war progressed, a tactic called the "creeping barrage" developed. The idea was for a curtain of shells to fall just ahead of advancing infantry. The aim was to keep the enemy pinned in their trenches. The creeping barrage relied on accurate artillery fire and good communications. This tactic was used with varying degrees of success, notably in the Battle of the Somme and the Second Battle of the Aisne.[4]

NEW IDEAS

The creeping barrage was one of many new ideas that were tried out and developed on the Western Front. Gas attacks, first attempted by the Germans, were widely used by both sides. Soldiers carried gas masks, but various different types of poison gas were responsible for thousands of deaths during the war.[5] The most astonishing "new idea" for the troops who watched it first drive into action in 1916 was the tank (see also pages 46–47). The other major innovation of World War I was the use of aircraft.

World War I broke out only a decade after the first successful powered flight. At the beginning of the war, aircraft were considered useful only for **reconnaissance**. Yet the pace of development of aircraft technology during the war was phenomenal. In 1914, France had fewer than 140 military planes. By 1918, it had around 4,500.[6] Planes were widely used on the Western Front for observation, often to guide artillery attacks.[7] But as the war progressed, small fighter aircraft (see panel on page 45) battled for control of the sky above the battlegrounds. Bigger planes that could carry bombs were used for ground attacks, and for some attacks on cities (see page 57).

△ Here, Baron von Richthofen can be seen in his fighter plane. Richthofen was Germany's top aviator during World War I, and was nicknamed The Red Baron.

Garros and Fokker

Fights in the air began fairly ineffectually, as pilots tried to fire at each other with small guns or rifles. The French pilot Roland Garros was the first to devise a way of protecting the plane's propeller with steel plates so that a machine gun could be fired forwards. His invention was successful, but his luck ran out when he was shot down in April 1917, and his plane was captured.[8] However, a Dutchman named Anthony Fokker, who was working for the Germans, came up with a better mechanism – the interrupter gear. This was a timing mechanism that prevented the gun from firing when a propeller blade was in front of it. It was used to great effect by the Germans, while the Allies scrambled to produce a similar mechanism.[9]

THE TANK

The tank was the Allies' secret weapon. Tanks made their first brief appearance at Flers, during the Battle of the Somme in 1916, but their first major role was in the Battle of Cambrai on 20 November 1917. In fact, both the British and the French independently developed their own tanks during World War I.

This British tank is climbing a slope at Wailly, France, on the Western Front in October 1917.

The tank was developed to break the deadlock of trench warfare. It could move over ground broken by shell holes and force its way through barbed wire. In Britain, the development of this new weapon, known then as a "landship", was championed by Winston Churchill who established a Landships Committee in 1915. The first prototype, known as "Little Willie", was followed by another, "Big Willie", in 1916. The requirements laid down for the finished tank were a minimum speed of 6.5 kilometres (4 miles) per hour, a range of 32 kilometres (20 miles), the ability to climb a 1.5-metre (5-foot) high parapet and to cross a 2.5-metre (8-foot) trench. It should also have two machine guns and be immune to the effects of small-arms fire.[10]

BATTLE OF CAMBRAI

The earliest tanks were extremely unreliable. The 36 tanks used in the attack at Flers terrified the German troops, who had not seen this new weapon before, but virtually all of them broke down.[11] By 1917, the British had 476 tanks available for the attack at Cambrai.[12] This attack was against the Hindenburg Line (see page 40), but the tanks showed their worth as they advanced with the infantry following behind. The author Arthur Conan Doyle described the scene in these words: "The long line of tanks magnified to monstrous size in the dim light of early dawn, the columns of infantry with fixed bayonets who followed them, all advancing in silent order, formed a spectacle which none who took part in it could ever forget."[13] Within hours, the tanks had crossed the fortifications of the Hindenburg Line, the first time the Allies had achieved this feat.[14]

Water carriers

The landship was developed and produced in conditions of utmost secrecy. The body shells of the vehicles looked rather like tanks that were used to carry water. So when the early models were being shipped to France, they were labelled as "'water carriers for Russia". It was shortened to "tank", and this was the name that stuck.[17]

For the crews inside the tanks, conditions were truly appalling. In the cramped, hot interior, the men suffered from the engine noise and exhaust fumes, and violent movements as the tank crossed broken ground. Many were violently sick or even lost consciousness. Nevertheless, the success of the tank at Cambrai prompted the Germans to develop their own models, although they produced very few compared to the numbers of tanks built by the Allies. On 24 April 1918, rival tanks met each other for the first time in the war at Villers-Bretonneux. The Allies used tanks for the final assaults on the Hindenburg Line in 1918.[15]

Tank Production 1916–1918[16]

Year	UK	France	Germany	Italy	USA
1916	150	-	-	-	-
1917	1,277	800	-	-	-
1918	1,391	4,000	20	6	84

THE USA ENTERS THE WAR

"If we end up at war with America, we will face an enemy with such moral, financial, and economic strength that we will have nothing more to hope for from the future; that is my firm conviction." These words were written by the German banker Max Warburg in January 1917, at a time when the pros and cons of unrestricted submarine warfare were being hotly debated in Germany (see page 31).[1] Warburg thought the risk of pushing the United States to declare war was too great, but only a small minority in Germany shared his opinion. The return to unrestricted submarine warfare on 1 February caused President Woodrow Wilson to break off diplomatic relations with Germany two days later. The sinking of several US merchant ships in the following weeks, as well as the Cunard liner the *Laconia*, brought the United States ever closer to declaring war.

THE ZIMMERMAN TELEGRAM

In February 1917, the British intelligence service passed to President Wilson a telegram that had been sent and intercepted in the previous month. It was from the German foreign minister, Arthur Zimmerman to the German minister in Mexico. In it, Zimmerman urged Mexico to attack the United States in alliance with Germany if the United States entered the war. The Zimmerman telegram was published on 1 March 1917 to great public outrage in the United States.[2] President Wilson declared war on Germany on 6 April 1917.

NEW OPERATIONS

For the Allies, the entry of the United States into the war was a relief. Germany's policy of unrestricted submarine warfare was alarmingly successful from an Allied point of view. The United States' entry into the war immediately mobilized the powerful US navy, but it was the introduction of the convoy system that curtailed the U-boats' activities. The success of the German U-boats did, however, prompt a new offensive on the Western Front. Britain's General Haig wanted to attack the German lines in Belgium, with the aim of breaking through and destroying the U-boat bases at Ostende and Zeebrugge. This aim led to the Third Battle of Ypres, also known as Passchendaele, which began on 31 July 1917. The fighting dragged on until November with a small gain for the Allies. Once again the cost in human life was enormous – 310,000 Allied and 260,000 German casualties.[3]

The French army played virtually no part in the Third Battle of Ypres. It was still recovering from the casualties of the Nivelle Offensive and the mutinies that followed (see page 41). The overall French strategy had changed from one of offence to defence.[4] As General Pétain said, "We must wait for the Americans and the tanks."

Mud

During the Third Battle of Ypres, heavy summer rain turned the ground to mud. This description of the battlefield was written by Private H. Jeary of the Queen's Royal West Surrey Regiment: "As far as the eye could see was a mass of black mud with shell holes filled with water. Here and there broken duckboards, partly submerged in the quagmire; here and there a horse's carcass sticking out of the water; here and there a corpse…"[5]

◁ Shell holes, filled with water and surrounded by a sea of mud, were a common sight at Ypres, 1917.

WOODROW WILSON

As president of the United States when war broke out in Europe in 1914, Woodrow Wilson adopted a stance of neutrality. He saw his role as one of peacemaker and worked actively throughout 1915 and 1916 to try to find a solution to the stalemate. In December 1916, Wilson sent identical peace notes to all the participants in the war, asking each one to state their terms for peace. In January 1917 he gave a speech to the US Senate in which he called for "peace without victory" and outlined his idea for a future league of nations.[6]

A FINE BALANCE

From 1914 to 1917, Wilson skilfully managed to keep his country neutral while continuing to trade with countries involved in the war, notably Great Britain. The Germans' response was to try to disrupt this trade with unrestricted submarine warfare, but they were treading a fine line because they did not want to provoke the United States into declaring war. The sinking of merchant ships and the Zimmerman telegram tipped this balance in 1917. On 2 April, Wilson went before Congress to call for a declaration of war. He told Congress that the time for neutrality was over and that "The world must be made safe for democracy." In this speech, Wilson made it clear that the United States was going to war for sound moral reasons. By taking the United States into the war, Wilson also hoped to have greater influence over what happened after it ended.

THE FOURTEEN POINTS

Wilson continued his diplomatic efforts even after the United States entered the war. In January 1918 he presented Congress with 14 points on which peace should be negotiated (see page 63 for a summarized list of the 14 points). The last of the points outlined the foundation of a "general association of nations" – the League of Nations – which would give a guarantee of "political independence and territorial integrity to great and small states alike".[7] After the **Armistice** in November 1918 (see page 64), Wilson went in person to Paris to take part in the negotiations for what he hoped would be an enduring peace after the war.

BIOGRAPHY

Thomas Woodrow Wilson 1856–1924

BORN: Staunton, Virginia, USA

ROLE: 28th president of the United States (1913–1921). In 1916, Wilson became the first **Democratic** president to win a second term in office since Andrew Jackson in 1832. His slogan as he ran for the presidency was "He kept us out of war", but his victory was also the result of social legislation, such as laws to prohibit child labour, and to limit the working day to eight hours for most railway workers.[8]

DID YOU KNOW? Woodrow Wilson's father was a Presbyterian minister who served as a chaplain for the Confederate Army in the Civil War. His church was turned into a military hospital, and the young Woodrow Wilson saw the horrors of war at first hand.[9]

THE AMERICAN EXPEDITIONARY FORCE

In April 1917, the USA had a powerful navy, but only a small army of around 108,000.[10] In order to supply the numbers of soldiers needed by the Allies, conscription was introduced in May 1917. The first US troops of the American Expeditionary Force arrived in France in June 1917 with their commander General John Pershing. Over the following months, thousands more US troops were recruited and trained. By March 1918, there were more than 300,000 US troops, known as "doughboys", on French soil.[11] Pershing was determined that the American Expeditionary Force should fight as a separate unit on the Western Front, not be broken up amongst the British and French troops. But the Allies became so desperate for manpower in the spring of 1918 that Pershing relented and released some troops to serve under British and French commanders as a temporary measure.

OPERATION MICHAEL

At the end of 1917, fighting on the Eastern Front came to an end and Russia opened peace negotiations with Germany. The Treaty of Brest-Litovsk between the Central Powers and Russia was signed on 3 March 1918. The commander of the German army, General Erich Ludendorff, began to transfer troops from the Eastern to the Western Front in preparation for one final, all-out attack on the British and the French. He was keen to launch this offensive before the Americans had time to get their troops battle-ready. The main part of Ludendorff's plan, codenamed "Michael", was to attack the British line on the Somme and push the British forces rapidly towards the English Channel. This would create a gap between the British and the French armies. Ludendorff calculated that if he could crush the British, the French would admit defeat.

Operation Michael began on 21 March 1918. The Germans rapidly broke through the British lines on the Somme and advanced more than 65 kilometres (40 miles). This was the biggest territorial gain on the Western Front since 1914. But the effort of advancing over the broken, devastated ground exhausted the battle-weary German soldiers. Ludendorff called off the attack in early April.

The Lafayette Escadrille

Although US soldiers did not start to arrive officially in France until 1917, many volunteers from the United States were already fighting in the war. Some served in the French Foreign Legion; others worked in the ambulance corps. From 1915, many US pilots enlisted in the French Air Service, and in 1916 they formed their own squadron – the Lafayette Escadrille. Members of the squadron fought over the battlefields of Verdun in 1916, and observed the German retreat to the Hindenburg Line in 1917. The squadron had two lion cubs named "Whiskey" and "Soda" as mascots. In all, 38 US pilots served in the Lafayette Escadrille, which became part of the American Air Service in 1917. The expertise of those pilots who had already flown on the Western Front was invaluable for the new US squadrons. The lion cubs, meanwhile, went to live in the zoo in Paris.[12]

△ Here, members of the Lafayette Escadrille are pictured with their lion cub mascots.

THE HOME FRONT

In Britain, almost the first act of the government after declaring war in 1914 was to pass the Defence of the Realm Act (DORA) on 8 August. This act gave the government wide-ranging powers, including the rights to seize property and resources for the war effort, to imprison without trial, and to censor and control information (see page 16).[1] This law was also used to control many aspects of civilian life, for example people were not permitted to light bonfires or set off fireworks, to ring church bells, or to buy binoculars.

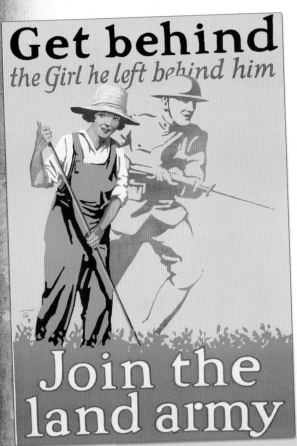

FOOD SHORTAGES

Food **rationing** was not introduced in Britain until 1918. In the first two years of the war, there were no real shortages of food. However, the start of unrestricted submarine warfare in 1915 did begin to have an effect on the supplies of food coming into the country. Another problem was that the number of men leaving their jobs to go and fight had left many farms short-handed. The Women's Land Army was set up in response to this. By 1917 there were over 260,000 women farm labourers.[2]

△ This recruiting poster for the Women's Land Army urges people to support women who volunteer to do agricultural work.

In December 1916, the government established a Ministry of Food, and acted to ensure that all suitable land was being cultivated in order to boost food production. Fears of food shortages and panic-buying finally led to the introduction of rationing in 1918. First sugar was rationed, then meat, followed by all basic commodities.

WOMEN AND THE WAR

The war opened up new opportunities for women in Britain and in the United States. Before the war, work considered suitable for women was limited. Large numbers of women were employed in **domestic service**. But as men left their jobs to volunteer for the army, women began to replace them in a wide range of occupations.[3] In Britain there was opposition from the unions and from those who did not think women capable of doing "men's jobs". But as the war continued, women took on work in areas ranging from clerical work and education to public transport, factory assembly lines, and ship-building.[4] Many women from the United States and Britain supported the war effort by nursing the wounded, or working as drivers or telephone operators.

Women and the vote

World War I broke out at a time when many women in Britain were campaigning for the right to vote. In the years before the war, this campaign had become increasingly violent. But the **suffragettes'** support for the war effort, and the valuable war work being carried out by women generally, did a huge amount to sway public opinion. In 1918, the Representation of the People Act gave the right to vote to women over 30 years old. It was not until 1928 that women had equal voting rights with men in Britain. In the United States, women achieved equal voting rights with men in 1920, again as a direct result of the major role played by women during the war.

THE MUNITIONETTES

One of the most notable areas in which women took a role during World War I was in the munitions factories. The amount of ammunition, particularly shells, being used on the Western Front created a crisis in the munitions industry in Britain in 1915.[5] In May 1915, the government created a new Ministry of Munitions headed by David Lloyd George and in June this ministry took direct control of the industry. Lloyd George forced employers to accept unskilled labour in order to boost production. Thousands of women, known as munitionettes, were employed.

The work in the munitions factories was hard and dangerous. The women handled explosives, such as **TNT**, and other chemicals without any protective clothing. The workers were nicknamed "canaries" because exposure to sulphur gave their skin a yellow colour. They were also paid far less than their male counterparts – on average less than half. The trade union leader Mary Macarthur led a campaign for better pay for the munitionettes, but by 1918 the situation was much the same.[6]

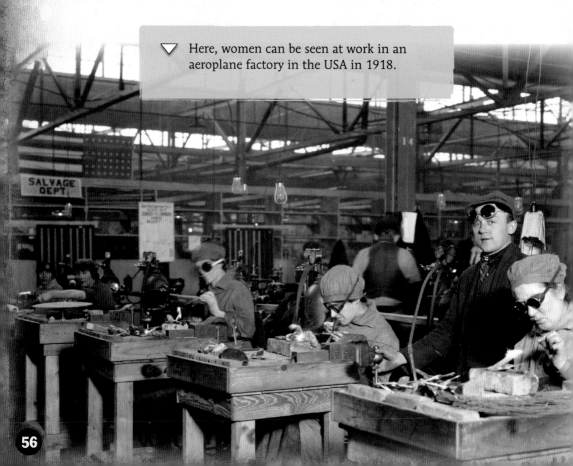

Here, women can be seen at work in an aeroplane factory in the USA in 1918.

Conchies

Some of the men who were called up to serve in the army refused to do so. They were called "conscientious objectors" (COs), or "conchies". Some opposed the war on political grounds, others on religious or moral grounds. There were about 16,000 COs in Britain during World War I. Some hardliners spent the war locked up in prison; others were prepared to work for the war effort as non-combatants. They were generally treated with great hostility by the general public.

ATTACKS ON THE HOME FRONT

The war came to the home front in Britain on 19 January 1915, when a zeppelin bombed Great Yarmouth and King's Lynn on the east coast. The raid killed two people and injured 16,[7] and it caused outrage that civilians were being targeted in this way. A zeppelin was a cigar-shaped airship powered by several engines, filled with hydrogen and therefore lighter than air. The Germans used their zeppelins for observation and, increasingly during 1915, for bombing raids.

The first raid on London was in May 1915, and it was followed by many others. The worst was on 8 September 1915, when a zeppelin bombed central London, causing huge amounts of damage. The raid was described by Beatrice Webb in her diaries: "From the balcony we could see shrapnel bursting over the river and behind, somewhat aimlessly. In another few minutes a long sinuous airship appeared high up in the blue black sky, lit up faintly by searchlights ... It moved slowly ... the shells bursting far below it – then there were two bursts that seemed nearly to hit it and it disappeared ... It was a gruesome reflection that while we were being pleasantly excited, men, women and children were being killed and maimed..."[8]

At first, British defences were inadequate against the zeppelin threat. But during 1916, improved ammunition – bullets that could rip a hole in the skin of the zeppelin then set fire to the hydrogen gas inside – were developed. The Germans called off the zeppelin raids in 1917, after 77 out of the fleet of 115 had been destroyed or disabled.[9] Raids over Britain continued, however, flown by bomber planes.

REPORTING AND PROPAGANDA

"If the people really knew, the war would be stopped tomorrow. But of course they don't – and can't know. The correspondents don't write and the censorship would not pass the truth." David Lloyd George to C.P. Scott of the *Manchester Guardian*.[10]

Picturing the fronts

The army forbade troops from carrying cameras on the Western Front. Yet some troops flouted the ban to take photographs, a few of which appeared in the newspapers. The government appointed official photographers for the Western Front and elsewhere, but they were subject to similar controls as the war reporters. In 1917, a photographer named Horace Nicholls was appointed as the first official photographer on the home front in Britain. His brief was to cover the civilian war effort and the role of women workers.[12] Official war artists were also appointed to depict the war. They included Paul Nash, C.R.W. Nevinson, and Eric Kennington.

REPORTING THE WAR

The newspapers in Britain were largely in favour of the war in 1914, and the two most powerful newspaper owners, Lord Northcliffe and Lord Rothermere, were powerful figures, close to many members of the government. Nevertheless, the government was quick to pass legislation to control all information about military activity, and to exercise censorship. In August 1914, the War Office Press Bureau was set up. This organization received news and information from the British army, censored it, and then passed it on to the press. The newspapers wanted to send their own reporters to the front, but this was refused. Instead, Lord Kitchener appointed Colonel Ernest Swinton to be the army's official journalist. His reports were censored, then vetted by Lord Kitchener himself before being released to the press under the byline "Eye Witness".[11]

Concern about these restrictions led the British government to allow selected journalists to become accredited war reporters in 1915. They wore uniforms and were escorted by army officials wherever they went. They were therefore in no position to report accurately or criticize military operations. Like the newspaper owners, they saw their job as very much part of the "war effort".[13]

PROPAGANDA

In Britain, war propaganda was carried out by various government departments including the War Propaganda Bureau (see page 16–17) until the establishment of the Department of Information in February 1917. Methods of propaganda included the recruiting posters that urged men to join up, as well as pamphlets, films, and even toys and comics for children.[14] Fear and loathing of the Germans was encouraged with stories of atrocities as the German armies advanced at the beginning of the war.[15]

In the United States, President Wilson was concerned about levels of public support for what was seen as a largely "European" war. Having fought and won an election on the byline "He kept us out of war", Wilson was now faced with the prospect of rallying public opinion to enter the war. In April 1917, he set up the Committee on Public Information (CPI) to promote the war to the American people. Under the leadership of a journalist named George Creel, the CPI used a wide range of propaganda in newspapers, on posters, on the radio, and in films to get its message across.[16]

Even children's toys had a part to play in wartime propaganda. This child stands proudly in front of a submarine go-kart.

THE END OF THE WAR

Throughout 1916, food and fuel shortages had become an increasing problem in Russia. Growing discontent led to strikes and demonstrations against the Tsar and his government as people demanded food. The Russian army, too, was exhausted and demoralized. In February 1917, troops in the Russian capital, Petrograd (St Petersburg), refused to fire on crowds of demonstrators. This "February Revolution" led to the abdication of Tsar Nicholas II (see page 27) and the establishment of a provisional government.[1]

THE OCTOBER REVOLUTION

The minister of war in the new government, Alexander Kerensky, believed that a victory on the Eastern Front would gain support for the provisional government. So, in June 1917, he launched a new offensive in Galicia against the Austrian army. Although the Russians had some initial success against the Austrians, they were soon brought to a standstill by German reinforcements. Thousands of Russian soldiers, weary of war, deserted their posts. Meanwhile, in Russia, the authority of the provisional government was being challenged by members of the **Bolshevik** Party, led by Vladimir Lenin. In October 1917, the Bolshevik Revolution overthrew the provisional government and marked the beginning of **communist** rule in Russia.

In his "Decree on Peace" (26 October) Lenin proposed a three-month ceasefire and a "just and democratic peace for which the great majority of wearied, tormented, and war-exhausted toilers and labouring classes of all belligerent countries are thirsting".[2] Lenin signed an armistice with the Central Powers on 15 December 1917, followed by the Treaty of Brest-Litovsk on 3 March 1918. Under the terms of the treaty, Russia renounced any claims over Finland and Ukraine, as well as the Baltic states and Poland. The Allies refused to participate in these peace negotiations and the treaty was, in fact, later **annulled** under the terms of the 1918 Armistice (see page 63).[3]

Vladimir Lenin
1870–1924

BORN: Simbirsk, Russia

ROLE: Founder of the Russian Communist Party and leader of the Bolshevik Revolution in 1917. He studied law, but was arrested for his revolutionary beliefs and sent to Siberia. After this he spent much time in exile in Europe. He became leader of the Bolshevik faction of the Social Democratic Worker's Party. His theories of government, together with those of Karl Marx, formed the backbone of communism. He led the October Revolution in 1917 and, after three years of civil war, the communist government of Soviet Russia.[4]

DID YOU KNOW? Lenin survived an assassination attempt in August 1918 by a member of the Socialist Revolutionary Party. In response, hundreds of political opponents were executed under Lenin's authorization.

THE BEGINNING OF THE END

On the Western Front, the Allies were sufficiently worried by the German gains in Operation Michael (see page 52) to allow the appointment of the French Chief of Staff Ferdinand Foch as supreme commander of the Allied forces. Ludendorff meanwhile persisted with his planned offensive, mounting attacks in Belgium in April, and threatening Paris in May. These attacks were initially successful, but the usual problems of keeping the troops supplied, as well as large numbers of casualties, resulted in Ludendorff calling a halt to both.[5]

THE LAST BATTLES

Ludendorff's last attack, the Second Battle of the Marne in July 1918, was his final, desperate attempt to break the Allies. It marked the beginning of the end for the German army. A series of counter-offensives mounted by the Allies started with an attack at Amiens on 8 August led by hundreds of French and British tanks. Ludendorff called this the "black day of the German army".[6] The Germans had reached the end of their resources just as US troops were beginning to arrive in huge numbers on the Western Front. US troops were first involved in an offensive in May at Catigny. They fought a successful battle at Le Hamel with Australian troops on 4 July. Then, in September, the American Expeditionary Force – this time working as an independent unit – achieved a spectacular victory at St Mihiel, south of Verdun.[7]

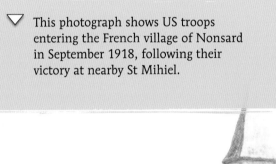

This photograph shows US troops entering the French village of Nonsard in September 1918, following their victory at nearby St Mihiel.

The Fourteen Points

In January 1918, President Woodrow Wilson presented the US Congress with 14 points on which the end of World War 1 should be negotiated.[9] This is a summary of those 14 points:

1. Open covenants of peace [peace treaties], openly arrived at.

2. Freedom of navigation on the seas outside territorial waters in peace and in war.

3. The removal of all economic barriers, and establishment of equality of trade.

4. Guarantees that national armaments will be reduced to the lowest point consistent with domestic safety.

5. A free, open-minded, and absolutely impartial adjustment of all colonial claims, that in determining all such questions ... the interests of the people concerned must have equal weight with the claims of the government whose title is to be determined.

6. The evacuation of all Russian territory.

7. Belgium should be evacuated and restored.

8. All French territory should be freed and the invaded portions restored, and the wrong done to France by Prussia in 1871 in the matter of Alsace-Lorraine ... should be righted...

9. The frontiers of Italy should be readjusted along clearly recognizable lines of nationality.

10. The peoples of Austria-Hungary should have the freest opportunity to independent development.

11. Romania, Serbia, and Montenegro should be evacuated and restored ... and the relations of the several Balkan states to each other should be determined by friendly counsel...

12. The Turkish portion of the Ottoman Empire should have a secure sovereignty, but the other nationalities which are under Turkish rule should have an undoubted security of life and an opportunity of independent development, and the Dardanelles should be permanently opened as passage to the ships and commerce of all nations.

13. An independent Polish state should be erected including the territories inhabited by Polish populations...

14. The League of Nations should be formed.

THE END OF THE GERMAN EMPIRE

By the end of September, Ludendorff and Hindenburg knew that there was no alternative but to seek an armistice. Peace notes were sent to President Wilson asking for the opening of peace negotiations based on the 14 Points. Meanwhile the fighting continued on the Western Front. Although the Allied troops had made significant advances across the Hindenburg Line, they continued to encounter strong resistance. In a complete change of heart, Ludendorff demanded that Germany should continue to fight. But it was too late, and on 26 October Ludendorff resigned.[8]

On 8 November, General Foch met the German armistice delegation on a special train in the Forest of Compiègne, near Paris. With revolution threatening on the streets of Germany's cities, the abdication of Kaiser Wilhelm II was announced on 9 November (signed and made official on 28 November) and Germany was proclaimed a **republic**.

THE ARMISTICE

The terms of the armistice were harsh. Germany was required to evacuate all occupied land, including Alsace-Lorraine, within two weeks, and to hand over large amounts of war equipment to the Allies. The Treaty of Brest-Livotsk and another treaty with Romania were annulled. Any deviation from the armistice terms would result in the resumption of hostilities within 48 hours. The German negotiators had little choice but to accept – Germany was in no state to carry on fighting. The armistice was signed at 5 a.m. on 11 November. The war came to an end at 11 a.m. on the same day.[10]

The Allies continued their blockade on Germany into 1919, while the negotiations at the Paris Peace Conference took place. The situation in Germany became desperate. In a telegram sent to Paris, Field Marshal Herbert Plumer, commander of the British Army of Occupation on the Rhine, said: "In my opinion food must be sent into this area by the Allies without delay. The mortality amongst women, children, and the sick is most grave, and sickness due to hunger is spreading. The attitude of the population is becoming one of despair, and the people feel that an end by bullets is preferable to death by starvation."[11] The full blockade only ended when the Treaty of Versailles was eventually signed, on 28 June (see page 66).

REMEMBRANCE THROUGH LITERATURE

Many of those who were caught up in the war wrote about their experiences, whether in diaries, letters or poems, or afterwards in **memoirs** and novels. As a young nurse, Vera Brittain tended wounded soldiers in England, Malta, and France. She lost her fiancé, her brother, and several friends in the fighting on the Western Front. In France, she often looked after German prisoners-of-war, and the realization of the terrible absurdity of war never left her. She became an active member of the peace movement after the war, and wrote one of the best memoirs of the war, *Testament of Youth* (1933), about her experiences, and about the people she had lost.[12] Like many others, Brittain did not feel that the Paris Peace Conference and the Treaty of Versailles was a satisfactory outcome to the war. She wrote, "When I thought about these negotiations at all ... they did not represent ... the kind of 'victory' that the young men whom I had loved would have regarded as sufficient justification for their lost lives..."[13]

Military casualties

There are no definitive figures for casualties during World War I, but these estimates show the scale of the conflict.[14]

Country	Killed	Wounded or missing
Belgium	44,000	450,000
Great Britain	659,000	2,391,000
France	1,359,000	4,455,000
Russia	1,700,000	5,000,000
United States	58,000	204,000
Austria-Hungary	922,000	3,620,000
Germany	1,600,000	4,168,000
Italy	689,000	959,000
India	43,000	71,000
Canada	57,000	150,000
Australia	58,000	152,000
Turkey	250,000	400,000

WHAT HAVE WE LEARNED?

In early 1919, Allied leaders met in Paris to decide on the terms for peace. It was this meeting that produced the Treaty of Versailles. Four heads of government – David Lloyd George of Britain, Georges Clemenceau of France, Woodrow Wilson of the United States, and Vittorio Orlando of Italy – effectively made all the decisions. The Allies all wanted something slightly different – Wilson envisaged a settlement based on his 14 points, including the establishment of a League of Nations that would provide **collective security**. Britain and France were keen to make the Germans pay for the war, and France was determined to achieve security against future aggression. The Germans themselves were given no say in the treaty that was presented to them in May 1919, and which they eventually signed in June.[1]

Total war: a new kind of conflict

It is clear that World War 1 was a very different kind of war from any experienced before. It was a world war because it involved troops from all parts of the globe, and because the fighting was widespread. It was also the first industrial war. Advances in weapons technology and industrial manufacturing allowed the slaughter of huge numbers of soldiers. The war swallowed up resources — not only the men fighting on the various battle fronts, but also the men and women on the home fronts, labouring to feed the war effort. The organization of entire societies around the needs of the war became known as "total war".

STABBED IN THE BACK?

The terms of the Treaty of Versailles caused huge resentment in Germany. It imposed a "War Guilt Clause" that allotted blame for the war to Germany and her allies, and as a consequence forced Germany to pay **reparations** – the final amount was not decided until 1921. In addition, Germany lost territory in Europe and overseas, its fleet was surrendered to Britain, conscription was banned, and its army was restricted to 100,000 men. The Allies knew that the Germans would not like the terms, but they calculated that in defeat, Germany had little choice.

The problem was that many Germans did not believe that their country had been defeated. No victorious armies had marched into Berlin. Instead, the German soldiers had returned home still looking very much like a fighting force. Encouraged by Ludendorff and others, rumours circulated that the army had been "stabbed in the back" – betrayed and robbed of certain victory by its own government under the influence of socialists and pacifists. These rumours, coupled with the terms of the treaty, provoked fury in Germany.[2]

TOWARDS WORLD WAR II

The Allies themselves disagreed about the treaty. In the United States, the Senate, under **Republican** control since the end of 1918, rejected the Treaty of Versailles and negotiated separate peace terms with the Germans. France wanted strict enforcement of the treaty's terms, while Britain adopted a more conciliatory approach. It is clear that this disunity between the Allies was a major factor in failing to contain German power, and allowing the rise of nationalism and militarism in Germany in the years that followed. In the 1930s, the rising Nazi leader Adolf Hitler violated the terms of the treaty many times, with little opposition from the Allies. The scene was set for the outbreak of another world war. Even in the 21st century, we are still dealing with problems created by the events of World War I and made worse after World War II – for example, the break up of the former Yugloslavia, and the impact of decisions made about Arab independence and a Jewish Homeland.

TIMELINE

PRE-WAR

1839 Treaty of Guarantee of Belgian neutrality
1871 Franco-Prussian War ends
1879 Austro-German Treaty
1882 Triple Alliance (Germany, Austria-Hungary and Italy)
1887 Reinsurance Treaty (Germany and Russia)
1888 Wilhelm II becomes Kaiser (Emperor) of German Empire
1890 Bismarck resigns
1894 Franco-Russian Alliance
1902 Anglo-Japanese Alliance
1904 *Entente Cordiale* (France and Britain)
1907 Anglo-Russian Agreement
1908 Bosnian annexation crisis
1912–1913 First and Second Balkan Wars

1914

28 June Archduke Franz Ferdinand assassinated in Sarajevo
23 July Austria-Hungarian ultimatum to Serbia
28 July Austro-Hungary declares war on Serbia
1 Aug Germany declares war on Russia
2 Aug Ultimatum from Germany to Belgium demanding safe passage across Belgian territory
3 Aug Germany declares war on France. German army invades Belgium.
4 Aug Britain declares war on Germany. President Woodrow Wilson declares US policy of neutrality.
6 Aug onwards Battle of the Frontiers (Western Front)
9–16 Aug BEF lands in France
17 Aug Russia invades East Prussia and has initial victory at Stalluponen (Eastern Front)
20 Aug Battle of Gumbinnen (Eastern Front).
23 Aug Battle of Mons (Western Front). Austria-Hungary invades Russian Poland (Eastern Front).
26–30 Aug Battle of Tannenberg (Eastern Front) ends with German victory
28 Aug Naval battle of Heligoland Bight
6–10 Sept Battle of the Marne ends with German retreat followed by "Race to the Sea" (Western Front)
9 Sept First Battle of the Masurian Lakes (Eastern Front)
18 Oct–12 Nov First Battle of Ypres ends with both sides dug into trenches along the Western Front
29 Oct Ottoman Empire enters the war on the side of the Central Powers
Dec–Mar 1915 French offensive in Champagne (Western Front)
25 December Unofficial Christmas truce in the trenches (Western Front)

1915

19 Jan First zeppelin raid on Britain
31 Jan First use of poison gas at Battle of Bolimov (Eastern Front)
4 Feb Germany declares unrestricted submarine warfare
7–21 Feb Second Battle of the Masurian Lakes (Eastern Front)
Feb Naval bombardment starts in Dardanelles Strait

10 Mar Offensive at Neuve Chapelle (Western Front)

22 April First use of poison gas on Western Front at Second Battle of Ypres (Western Front)

25 Apr Allied landings in Gallipoli

7 May *Lusitania* is sunk by a German U-boat

1 Sept Germany suspends unrestricted submarine warfare

7 Dec British government orders evacuation of all troops from Gallipoli

1916

21 February Start of Battle of Verdun (Western Front)

31 May Naval Battle of Jutland

4 June Brusilov Offensive (Eastern Front)

1 July–19 Nov Battle of the Somme (Western Front)

1917

1 Feb Germany resumes unrestricted submarine warfare

Feb-Apr German withdrawal to the Hindenburg Line

26 Feb Russian troops refuse to fire on demonstrators in Petrograd

1 March Publication of the Zimmerman telegram

15 March Abdication of Tsar Nicholas II

3 Apr Lenin arrives in Petrograd

6 Apr USA declares war on Germany

9 Apr Nivelle Offensive starts with Battle of Arras. Canadian troops capture Vimy Ridge (Western Front).

Apr–May Failure of Nivelle Offensive results in mutiny in the French army

10 May First use of convoy system to protect merchant shipping

June First US troops arrive in France

June Kerensky Offensive (Eastern Front)

31 July–Nov Start of Third Battle of Ypres (Passchendaele) (Western Front)

24 Oct October Revolution in Russia

20 Nov First mass use of tanks at Battle of Cambrai (Western Front)

15 Dec Lenin signs armistice with Central Powers

1918

8 January President Woodrow Wilson makes "14 points" speech

3 March Treaty of Brest-Litovsk between the Central Powers and Russia

21 March Start of German offensive "Operation Michael" (Western Front)

3 Apr French Chief of Staff Ferdinand Foch appointed supreme commander of Allied forces

4 July Australian and US troops defeat Germans at Battle of Hamel (Western Front)

15 July Start of Second Battle of the Marne (Western Front)

16–17 July Tsar Nicholas and family assassinated by Bolsheviks

8 Aug Allied attack at Amiens (Western Front)

12 Sept US forces achieve victory at St Mihiel (Western Front)

8 Nov General Foch meets German armistice delegation in Forest of Compiègne, near Paris

9 Nov Kaiser Wilhelm II abdicates (signed 28 Nov)

11 Nov Armistice signed and fighting ends at 11 a.m.

1919

Jan Start of Paris Peace Conference

28 June Signing of Treaty of Versailles

GLOSSARY

abdicate formally give up a throne

alliance union between two groups or countries

Allies Allied Powers, also called the Entente Powers. In World War I, the alliance of Britain (and the British Empire), France, and Russia. Other countries who fought with the Allies included Belgium, Serbia, Italy, Japan, Greece, and Romania. The United States never formally joined the alliance, remaining an "Associated Power".

annexation act of taking over and incorporating territory

annul declare something invalid

armistice agreement to stop fighting for an agreed length of time

artillery large guns that fire shells

attrition process of weakening or exhausting by constant pressure or harassment

autocratic type of rule by someone who has absolute power

Balkans region in south-eastern Europe with the Adriatic Sea to the west, the Mediterranean to the south, and the Black Sea to the east

bayonet sharp blade that can be fixed to the end of a rifle

beachhead area of shore in enemy territory secured and defended by landing forces

blockade act of preventing goods and food from entering a particular place

Bolshevik member of the group that split from the Russian Social Democratic Worker's Party in 1903. The Bolsheviks were led by Vladimir Lenin.

bombardment continuous attack with bombs or shells

cavalry soldiers on horseback

censorship act of removing information, for example, from a newspaper or a letter, that is considered to be unacceptable in some way

Central Powers in World War I, the alliance of Germany and Austria-Hungary, later joined by the Ottoman Empire and Bulgaria

Chief of Staff senior officer in a large organization, such as one of the armed forces

collective security global arrangement designed to prevent or stop wars. Each state in the system agrees that any aggression towards one state is considered to be aggression to all the states, which will then work together to respond to the threat. The League of Nations and the United Nations were founded on the principle of collective security.

colony country or region that is under the control of another country

communist person who believes in Communism, the political theory in which all property is owned by the community and each person contributes and receives according to his or her ability and needs

conscription compulsory service in the armed forces

convoy in World War I, the system used from 1917 onwards to protect merchant ships from U-boat attacks by grouping them together and surrounding them with a protective ring of naval ships

counter-attack attack made in response to one made by the enemy

decoy something used to imitate something else, in order to mislead

Democrat in the USA, a member of the centre-left Democratic Party

division in the armed forces, a large unit usually made up of several regiments or brigades

domestic service paid work in an employer's home, for example, as a cook, butler, or housemaid

dreadnought name given to the large, big-gun battleships developed in the run-up to World War I

grenade small bomb that is thrown by hand

imperialism dominance, often by use of military force, of a powerful state over another, usually weaker, state

leave time away from fighting or military work

memoir historical account written from personal experience

mine type of bomb that is placed just below the surface of the ground, or of the sea, that explodes on impact

mobilization act of preparing and organizing troops for active service

munitions military weapons and ammunition

mutiny rebellion against authority, particularly in the armed forces

nationalist person or movement with strong patriotic feelings

neutral not supporting either side in a conflict

no man's land in World War I, the area in between the opposing frontline trenches

offensive military campaign of attack

Ottoman Empire empire that was founded around 1300 by a Turkish prince, Osman, which lasted until 1922. From 1453 its capital was Constantinople (Istanbul).

pacifist person who believes that war and violence cannot be justified

parapet protective wall along the top of a trench

pincer being approached or squeezed from two sides

power bloc group of countries that together hold particular influence

propaganda information that is used to promote a political cause or point of view

rationing act of allowing each person to have only a fixed amount of food or other commodities

reconnaissance scouting out an area to gain information

reparations compensation paid for war damage

republic state with a form of government that is controlled by the people

Republican in the USA, a member of the centre-right Republican Party

sniper person who shoots very accurately across a long range from a hidden position

socialism political theory that is based on public ownership and cooperative management of resources

suffragette woman who demanded the right to vote through organized protest

tear gas type of gas that causes severe irritation to the eyes

TNT (trinitrotoluene) yellow-coloured high explosive

torpedo underwater missile that explodes when it hits its target

treaty formal agreement

trench mortar short gun that fires bombs

tsar name used for the kings of the Russian empire

vaporize turn into vapour

NOTES ON SOURCES

The War's Origins (pages 4–9)

1. www.britannica.com/
EBchecked/topic/66989/Otto-
von-Bismarck/9612/Imperial-
chancellor?anchor=ref150183
2. Frank McDonough, *Cambridge
Perspectives in History: The Origins of
the First and Second World Wars*, CUP
1997, 4
3. www.britannica.com/EBchecked/
topic/126237/colonialism
4. Colin Nicolson, *The Longman
Companion to The First World War
Europe 1914-1918*, Longman 2001, 8
5. Rickard, J (24 September 2007),
*German Battleship Classes of the First
World War*, www.historyofwar.org/
articles/lists_battleship_classes_
German_WWI.html
6. Niall Ferguson, *The Pity of War*,
Penguin 1998, 84
7. Nicolson, 26
8. ibid
9. www.royal-navy.mod.uk/history/
ships/hms-dreadnought-1906/index.
htm
10. www.bbc.co.uk/history/british/
britain_wwone/invasion_ww1_01.
shtml#four
11. Nicolson, 27
12. Ferguson, 84

1914 (pages 10–17)

1. Ferguson, 146
2. John Keegan, *The First World War*,
Hutchinson 1998, 56
3. www.srpska-mreza.com/bookstore/
kosovo/kosovo19.htm
4. McDonough, 15
5. www.firstworldwar.com/source/
austrianultimatum.htm
6. Nicolson, 79
7. ibid, 63
8. McDonough, 10
9. Nicolson, 95
10. www.1914-1918.net/regular.htm

11. Nicolson, 96
12. David Roberts, *Minds at War: The
Poetry and Experience of the First
World War*, Saxon Books 1999, 45
13. www.firstworldwar.com/source/
asquithspeechtoparliament.htm
14. Ferguson, 177
15. www.spartacus.schoolnet.co.uk/
FWWudc.htm
16. www.nationalarchives.gov.uk/
pathways/firstworldwar/first_world_
war/britain_outbreak_war.htm
17. Peter Vansittart, *Voices from the Great
War*, Penguin 1983, 28
18. Roberts, 54
19. H G Wells, The War That Will End
War, Frank & Cecil Palmer, 1914, 8
20. www.firstworldwar.com/posters/
uk.htm
21. www.1914-1918.net/kitcheners.htm
22. Ferguson, 198

The Dardanelles and Gallipoli (pages 18–21)

1. www.firstworldwar.com/timeline/
1914.htm
2. www.nationalarchives.gov.uk/path
ways/firstworldwar/battles/gallipoli.
htm
3. Nicolson, 120
4. Nicolson, 123
5. Keegan, 269
6. www.awm.gov.au/commemoration/
anzac/anzac_tradition.asp
7. www.bbc.co.uk/history/worldwars/
wwone/australia_01.shtml
8. www.anzacsite.gov.au/5environment/
vc/biography.html
9. www.anzacsite.gov.au/5environment/
vc/jakka.html
10. www.anzacsite.gov.au/5environment/
vc/biography.html

The Eastern Front (pages 22–27)
1. Norman Stone, *The Eastern Front 1914-1917*, Penguin 1998, 33
2. Stone, 35
3. ibid, 40, 43
4. Ferguson, 96
5. Stone, 17
6. ibid, 23, 49
7. www.britannica.com/EBchecked/ topic/648646/World-War-I
8. Nicolson, 106
9. Keegan, 107
10. www.firstworldwar.com/battles/ masurian1.htm
11. Nicolson, 108
12. Keegan, 185
13. ibid, 186
14. www.historyofwar.org/articles/ battles_bolimov.html
15. Nicolson, 110
16. ibid, 111
17. www.firstworldwar.com/source/ willynicky.htm

The war at sea (pages 28–33)
1. www.britannica.com/EBchecked/ topic/648646/World-War-I
2. Nicholson, 64
3. www.britannica.com/EBchecked/ topic/648646/World-War-I
4. Keegan, 285–6
5. www.firstworldwar.com/battles/ heliogoland.htm
6. Keegan, 285
7. Keegan, 286
8. www.firstworldwar.com/features/ lusitania.htm
9. Keegan, 287
10. Nicolson, 125
11. Keegan, 290
12. www.britannica.com/EBchecked/ topic/648646/World-War-I
13. ibid
14. www.iwm.org.uk/searchlight/server. php?show=nav.24361&do=media
15. www.iwm.org.uk/searchlight/server. php?show=nav.24361
16. www.uboat.net/history/wwi/part3. htm
17. ibid
18. www.uboat.net/wwi/men/ commanders/10.html
19. Spiegel, Adolf K.G.E. von, U-boat 202 (1919)

The Western Front (pages 34–41)
1. Keegan, 197
2. ibid, 207
3. ibid, 211
4. ibid, 214
5. www.black-history.org.uk/ pavilionindian.asp
6. Lyn MacDonald, *1915: The Death of Innocence*, Penguin 1993, 66
7. www.westernfrontassociation.com/ great-war-on-land/43-britain- allies/252-indian-army-western- front.html
8. www.bbc.co.uk/history/worldwars/ wwone/india_wwone_01.shtml
9. www.westernfrontassociation.com/ great-war-on-land/113-general- interest/810-labour-corps-pioneers. html
10. www.brighton-hove-rpml.org.uk/ HistoryAndCollections/ collectionsthemes/ pavilionindianhospitalart photography/Pages/home.aspx
11. Alistair Horne, *The Price of Glory Verdun 1916*, Penguin 1993, 36
12. Keegan, 300
13. ibid, 304
14. www.britannica.com/EBchecked/topic /251766/Douglas-Haig-1st-Earl-Haig
15. Keegan, 317
16. ibid, 349
17. www.westernfrontassociation.com/ great-war-on-land/65-germany- allies/235-germ-hind-line.html
18. www.firstworldwar.com/battles/ aisne2.htm
19. Wilfred Owen, "Exposure", George Walter (ed.), *The Penguin Book of First World War Poetry*. Penguin 2006, 55.

The changing nature of warfare (pages 42–47)
1. www.firstworldwar.com/atoz/rats.htm
2. www.firstworldwar.com/diaries/ awirelessoperator.htm
3. www.firstworldwar.com/weaponry/ machineguns.htm
4. www.firstworldwar.com/atoz/ creepingbarrage.htm
5. www.firstworldwar.com/weaponry/ gas.htm

6. www.theaerodrome.com/aircraft/
statistics.php
7. www.firstworldwar.com/airwar/
observation.htm
8. www.firstworldwar.com/airwar/
deflectorgear.htm
9. www.firstworldwar.com/bio/
fokker.htm
10. www.firstworldwar.com/weaponry/
tanks.htm
11. Keegan, 320
12. www.1914-1918.net/bat21.htm
13. www.firstworldwar.com/source/
cambrai_conandoyle.htm
14. www.firstworldwar.com/battles/
cambrai.htm
15. www.1914-1918.net/tanks.htm
16. www.firstworldwar.com/weaponry/
tanks.htm
17. www.national-army-museum.ac.uk/
exhibitions/permanent-galleries/
world-wars-1905-1945/did-you-know

**The USA enters the war (pages
48–53)**
1. Ferguson, 284
2. Nicolson, 197
3. www.firstworldwar.com/battles/
ypres3.htm
4. Nicolson, 102
5. Lyn MacDonald, *1914–1918: Voices
and Images of the Great War*, Penguin
1991, 255
6. Nicolson, 224
7. www.firstworldwar.com/source/
fourteenpoints.htm
8. millercenter.org/president/keyevents/
wilson
9. www.woodrowwilson.org/index.php/
woodrow-wilson-biography
10. Keegan, 379
11. Keegan, 401
12. www.neam.org/lafescweb/index.html

The Home Front (pages 54–59)
1. www.bbc.co.uk/history/trail/wars_
conflict/home_front/the_home_
front_05.shtml
2. www.spartacus.schoolnet.co.uk/
Wland.htm
3. www.bbc.co.uk/history/british/
britain_wwone/women_
employment_01.shtml

4. www.makingthemodernworld.org.
uk/stories/the_age_of_the_mass/04.
ST.01/?scene=6
5. Nicolson, 156
6. www.spartacus.schoolnet.co.uk/
Wmunitions.htm
7. www.firstworldwar.com/airwar/
bombers_zeppelins.htm
8. www.bbc.co.uk/history/trail/wars_
conflict/home_front/the_home_
front_06.shtml
9. www.nationalarchives.gov.uk/
education/lesson32.htm
10. Ferguson, 213
11. ibid, 223
12. www.iwm.org.uk/upload/
package/95/collections/
photographs/1914-1919.html
13. www.bbc.co.uk/history/british/
britain_wwone/war_media_01.shtml
14. Ferguson, 228
15. ibid, 232
16. www.firstworldwar.com/features/
propaganda.htm

The end of the war (pages 60–65)
1. www.britannica.com/EBchecked/
topic/648646/World-War-I
2. www.bbc.co.uk/history/worldwars/
wwone/eastern_front_01.shtml
3. Nicolson, 223
4. www.bbc.co.uk/history/historic_
figures/lenin_vladimir.shtml
www.britannica.com/EBchecked/
topic/335881/Vladimir-Ilich-Lenin
5. Nicolson, 104
6. Keegan, 442
7. www.spartacus.schoolnet.co.uk/
FWWmihiel.htm
8. Keegan, 446
9. Nicolson, 224
10. Keegan, 447
11. www.ashatteredpeace.com/chapter9.
html
12. www.oucs.ox.ac.uk/ww1lit/
collections/brittain
13. Roberts, 347
14. www.firstworldwar.com/features/
casualties.htm

What have we learned? (pages 66–67)
1. www.bbc.co.uk/history/worldwars/
wwone/versailles_01.shtml
2. ibid

BIBLIOGRAPHY

BOOKS

Arthur, Max. *Last Post*. London: Penguin 2006.

Cave, Nigel. *Vimy Ridge: Arras*. Barnsley: Leo Cooper 1997.

Ferguson, Niall. *The Pity of War*. London: Penguin 1998.

Giddings, Robert. *The War Poets*. London: Bloomsbury 1988.

Holt, Tonie and Valmai. *Major and Mrs Holt's Battlefield Guide to Ypres Salient*. Barnsley: Leo Cooper, 2000.

Horne, Alistair. *The Price of Glory: Verdun 1916*. London: Penguin 1993.

Keegan, John. *The First World War*. London: Hutchinson 1998.

Macdonald, Lyn. *1914-1918 Voices and Images of the Great War*. London: Penguin 1991.

MacDonald, Lyn. *1915 The Death of Innocence*. London: Penguin 1993.

MacDonald, Lyn. *The Roses of No Man's Land*. London: Penguin 1993.

MacDonald, Lyn. *They Called it Passchendaele*. London: Penguin 1993.

McDonough, Frank. Cambridge Perspectives in History: *The Origins of the First and Second World Wars*. Cambridge: CUP 1997.

Middlebrook, Martin. *The First Day on the Somme 1 July 1916*. London: Penguin 1984.

Middlebrook, Martin and Mary. *The Somme Battlefields*. London: Penguin 1994.

Nicolson, Colin. *The Longman Companion to The First World War Europe 1914-1918*. London: Longman 2001.

Noakes, Vivien. *Voices of Silence*. Stroud: Sutton Publishing 2006.

Reed, Paul. *Walking the Salient*. Barnsley: Leo Cooper 1999.

Roberts, David. *Minds at War The Poetry and Experience of the First World War*. Chicago: Saxon Books 1999.

Stone, Norman. *The Eastern Front 1914-1917*. London: Penguin 1998.

Vansittart, Peter. *Voices from the Great War*. London: Penguin 1983.

WEBSITES

www.bbc.co.uk/history/worldwars

www.firstworldwar.com/index.htm

www.nationalarchives.gov.uk/pathways/firstworldwar

www.1914-1918.net

www.battlefield-tours.com/index.htm

FIND OUT MORE

BOOKS

General World War I history

Barber, Nicola. *Questioning History: The Western Front*. London: Wayland 2003.

Brocklehurst, Ruth and Henry Brook. *The Usborne Introduction to the First World War*. London: Usborne Books 2007.

Howard, Michael. *The First World War: A Very Short Introduction*. Oxford: OUP 2007.

The role of women in World War I

Atkinson, Dr Diane. *Elsie and Mairi Go to War: Two Extraordinary Women on the Western Front*. London: Arrow 2010.

Storey, Neil and Molly Housego. *Women in the First World War*. London: Shire Publications 2010.

Memoirs and fiction about World War I

Brittain, Vera. *Testament of Youth*. London: Virago 1933.

Eldridge, Jim. *The Trenches – a First World War Soldier 1914-1918*. London: Scholastic 2008.

Morpurgo, Michael. *War Horse*. Glasgow: Egmont 2007.

Skirth, Ronald. *The Reluctant Tommy: An Extraordinary Memoir of the First World War*. London: Macmillan 2010.

Stewart, Capt Alexander and Cameron Stewart. *A Very Unimportant Officer: Life and Death on the Somme and at Passchendaele*. London: Hodder 2009.

Wilding, Valerie. *Road to War – a First World War Girl's Diary 1916-1917*. London: Scholastic 2008.

The poetry and poets of World War I

Barber, Nicola and Patrick Lee-Browne. *Poets of the First World War*. London: Evans 2001.

Dowswell, Paul. *History through Poetry: World War I*. London: Wayland 2002.

WEBSITES

www.1914-1918.net
This website is about the British Army in World War I. It gives detailed information about the army and soldiers' experiences.

www.bbc.co.uk/schools/worldwarone
This BBC web page has lots of information about World War I, including letters, diary extracts, and newspaper cuttings.

www.anzacsite.gov.au/5environment/vc/biography.html
This is an Australian government website about Gallipoli and the Anzac troops.

www.uboat.net/index.html
This website is about German U-boats in both world wars.

www.westernfrontassociation.com
This is the website of the Western Front Association.

www.neam.org/lafescweb/index.html
This website contains information about the Lafayette Escadrille.

www.wilfredowen.org.uk/home
www.oucs.ox.ac.uk/ww1lit
These websites are about the poets and poetry of World War I.

www.battle-of-jutland.com
Visit this website to find out more about the the Battle of Jutland, the largest sea battle in history.

www.firstworldwar.com/battles/if.htm
The Italian front took place in the mountainous region along the frontier between Italy and Austria.

www.firstworldwar.com/battles/mf.htm
www.turkeyswar.com/index.html
The Mesopotamian front – battles between the Ottoman Empire and Britain – took place in the region that is now Iraq.

INDEX

14 Points 50, 62, 63, 66

aircraft 44–45
  airships 57
  bomber planes 44, 57
  fighter planes 44, 45
  reconaissance 44
Allies *see* Britain; France;
  Russia
Alsace-Lorraine 4, 13,
  63, 64
Anzac troops 18–19,
  20–21, 62
armies
  American 52, 62
  British 14, 17, 34,
    34–35, 39–40, 49, 52
  French 13, 14, 34,
    38–39, 40–41, 49
  German 12, 13, 14, 15,
    23–24, 34–35, 38–41,
    49, 52, 62, 67
  Russian 22–25, 60
Armistice 50, 60, 62, 64
Arnauld de la Perière,
  Lothar von 33
artillery 43, 44
Asquith, Herbert 16
attrition, policy of 15, 39
Austria-Hungary 4, 6, 7,
  11, 22, 24, 25, 60, 63

Balkans 4, 7
battles
  of the Aisne (First) 15
  of the Aisne (Second)
    41, 44
  of Arras 40–41, 43
  of Bolimov 24
  of Cambrai 46, 47
  of the Frontiers 13
  of Le Hamel 62
  of the Marne (First) 14
  of the Marne (Second) 62
  of the Masurian Lakes
    (First) 23
  of the Masurian Lakes
    (Second) 24
  of Mons 14
  of Neuve Chapelle
    34–35

of St Mihiel 62
  of the Somme 39–40,
    44, 46
  of Tannenberg 23
  of Verdun 38–39, 40, 53
  of Ypres (First) 15, 36
  of Ypres (Second) 35
  of Ypres (Third -
    Passchendaele) 39, 49
  see also naval battles
Belgium 12, 13, 49, 61, 63
Bismarck, Otto von 4, 5
Black Hand 11
Bolsheviks 60, 61
bombing raids 44, 57
Bosnia 7, 10
Britain
  declares war 13, 16
  empire 6, 14
  home front 54–59
  pre-war 6, 12–13
  see also armies; navies
Brittain, Vera 65
Brusilov Offensive 25
Bulgaria 7, 19
Bülow, Bernhard von 5

casualties
  Allies 19, 25, 34, 35, 40,
    41, 49, 65
  Central Powers 49, 65
cavalry 22, 36
censorship 16, 54, 58
Central Powers *see*
    Austria-Hungary;
    Bulgaria; Germany;
    Ottoman Empire
Churchill, Winston 18,
    19, 46
Clemenceau, Georges 66
code-breaking 29
colonial troops 14, 36–37
colonies 5, 6, 8, 14, 63
communications,
    battlefield 42–43, 44
communism 60, 61
conscientious objectors 57
conscription 17, 52, 67
convoy system 31, 48
creeping barrage 44

Danilov, General Yuri 22
Dardanelles 18–19, 20
Defence of the Realm Act
    (DORA) 16, 54
dreadnoughts 8–9

East Prussia 22–23, 24
Eastern Front 22–25, 34,
    52, 60
Egypt 6, 36

Falkenhayn, General Erich
    von 14, 24, 34, 38, 39
Fisher, Admiral Sir John 8
Foch, Marshal Ferdinand
    61, 62
Fokker, Anthony 45
food production 54–55
food rationing 54, 55
France
    air power 44, 53
    mutinies 41
    Nivelle Offensive 40–41,
      49
    pre-war 4, 5, 6
    see also armies
Franco-Prussian War 4
Franz Ferdinand, Archduke
    10–11
French army 13
French Foreign Legion 53
"front line" 42

Galicia 24, 60
Gallipoli 18–19, 20
Garros, Roland 45
gas attacks 24, 35, 44
Germany
    blockade of 28, 29, 64
    declares war 12
    empire 5, 8
    postwar 67
    pre-war 4–5, 6, 7
    Schlieffen Plan 12, 13,
      14, 22
    surrender 62
    war reparations 67
    see also armies; navies
Greece 7
Grey, Sir Edward 12, 16

Haig, Field Marshal Douglas 39, 48–49
Herzegovina 7
Hindenburg, Field Marshal Paul von 23, 24, 40, 62
Hindenburg Line 40, 47, 53, 62
Hitler, Adolf 67

imperialism 6
Indian soldiers 36–37
intelligence services 29, 31
Italy 4, 6, 63

Jacka, Albert 20–21
Japan 6, 22, 26–27
Joffre, General Joseph 34
journalism 58–59

Kiel Canal 8
Kitchener, Lord 14, 17, 19, 58

Labour Corps 37
Lafayette Escadrille 53
League of Nations 50, 63, 66
Lenin, Vladimir 60, 61
literature 41, 65
Lloyd George, David 56, 58, 66
Ludendorff, General Erich von 40, 52, 61, 62, 67
Lusitania, sinking of 30

Manchuria 26, 27
mines 29, 40
Moltke, Helmuth von 13, 14
Montenegro 7, 63
Morocco 6, 7
munitions factories 56
mutinies 41

nationalism 4, 10, 11, 67
naval battles
    Dogger Bank 29
    Heligoland 28, 29
    Jutland 31
    prize rules 32, 33
naval blockades 28, 31
navies
    American 48, 52
    British 6, 8–9, 18, 28–29, 31, 32
    German 5, 6, 8, 9, 28–29, 30–31, 32
    Russian 22, 26–27
Nicholas II, Tsar 26, 27, 60

Nivelle, General Robert 40, 41
"no man's land" 42

Operation Michael 52, 61
Orlando, Vittorio 66
Ottoman Empire 4, 7, 18, 63

pacifism 16, 57
Paris Peace Conference 64, 65, 66
patriotism 16
Pershing, General John 52
Pétain, General Philippe 39, 41, 49
photographers 58
Poland 24, 60, 63
power blocs 6
Princep, Gavrilo 11
prisoners of war 25, 65
propaganda 16–17, 59

Q-ships (decoy ships) 33

"race to the sea" 15
radio 43
Rasputin, Grigori 27
Rennenkampf, General Paul 22, 23
Romania 63, 64
Royal British Legion 39
Russell, Bertrand 16
Russia 4, 5, 6, 7, 11, 12, 14, 52
    Brusilov Offensive 25
    Eastern Front 22–25
    revolution 25, 27, 60
    Romanov family 26–27, 60
    see also armies; navies

Samsonov, General Alexander 22, 23
Sarajevo 10
Sassoon, Siegfried 41
Schlieffen Plan 12, 13, 14, 22
scorched earth policy 40
Serbia 7, 10, 11, 13, 63
ships
    dreadnoughts 8–9
    Lusitania 30
    Q-ships (decoy ships) 33
    U-boats 29, 30, 31, 32–33, 48
snipers 42
social legislation 5, 51
socialism 5

submarine warfare 29, 30, 31, 32–33, 48, 50, 54

tanks 44, 46–47
telephone systems 43
Tirpitz, Alfred von 5, 8
total war 66
treaties
    Anglo-Japanese 6
    of Brest-Litovsk 52, 60, 64
    Entente Cordiale 6
    Reinsurance Treaty 4, 5
    of Versailles 64, 65, 66–67
trench warfare 15, 34, 42, 46
Triple Alliance 4, 6
Triple Entente 6
Turkey 4, 7, 18, 20, 63

USA
    American Expeditionary Force 52, 62
    enters the war 48, 50, 53
    navy 48, 52
    neutrality 50
    public support for the war 59
    women's war work 55
    see also armies; navies

volunteers 14, 17, 53

war artists 58
weapons 24, 33, 35, 44, 45, 46, 47, 56,
Wells, H.G. 17
Western Front 15, 34–43, 52, 61, 62
Wilhelm I, Kaiser 4
Wilhelm II, Kaiser 4–5, 6, 8, 9, 11, 14, 29, 62
Wilson, Woodrow 48, 50–51, 59, 62, 66
women
    voting rights 55
    war work 54, 55, 56
Women's Land Army 54
World War I
    armistice 50, 60, 62, 64
    origins 4–7, 10–11
    outbreak 11–13
    peace negotiations 50, 62, 63, 64

zeppelins 57
Zimmerman telegram 48, 50